BARGELLO QUILTS

with a twist

Maggie Ball

BARGELLO QUILTS

with a twist

Maggie Ball

CINCINNATI, OHIO

www.MyCraftivity.com

Connect. Create. Explore.

Published by KP Craft Books, an imprint of F+W Publications, Inc., 4700 East Galbraith Road, Cincinnati, Ohio, 45236. (800) 289-0963. First Edition.

Other fine Krause Publications titles are available from your local bookstore, craft supply store, online retailer or visit our website at www.fwpublications.com.

12 11 10 09 08   5 4 3 2 1

Distributed in Canada by Fraser Direct
100 Armstrong Avenue
Georgetown, ON, Canada L7G 5S4
Tel: (905) 877-4411

Distributed in the U.K. and Europe by David & Charles
Brunel House, Newton Abbot, Devon, TQ12 4PU, England
Tel: (+44) 1626 323200, Fax: (+44) 1626 323319
Email: postmaster@davidandcharles.co.uk

Distributed in Australia by Capricorn Link
P.O. Box 704, S. Windsor NSW, 2756 Australia
Tel: (02) 4577-3555

Library of Congress Cataloging-in-Publication Data

Ball, Maggie.
  Bargello quilts with a twist / Maggie Ball. -- 1st ed.
      p. cm.
  Includes index.
ISBN-13: 978-0-89689-597-3 (pbk. : alk. paper)
1. Strip quilting--Patterns. 2. Patchwork--Patterns. 3. Patchwork quilts. I. Title.
  TT835.B2636 2008
  746.46'041--dc22 2008031231

Editor: Nancy Breen
Designer: Nicole Armstrong
Production Coordinator: Matt Wagner
Photographers: Kris Kandler and Mark Frey

METRIC CONVERSION CHART		
To Convert	**To**	**Multiply By**
Inches	Centimeters	2.54
Centimeters	Inches	0.4
Feet	Centimeters	30.5
Centimeters	Feet	0.03
Yards	Meters	0.9
Meters	Yards	1.1

Purple Passion Pieced by Carol McKim.

DEDICATED TO

NIGEL, HAZEL & THOMAS

Acknowledgments

I'd like to thank everyone who has helped me on this book-writing adventure. I've had great support from the Krause Publications team, notably Erica Swanson and Nancy Breen, my editors; acquisitions editor Candy Wiza; Kris Kandler, the photographer, and Nicole Armstrong, the designer. David Textiles Inc. generously provided fabric for many of the quilts. Computer software from The Electric Quilt Company® was invaluable for designing the projects. Mark Frey photographed the quilts that I couldn't send to Krause. Twenty-three of my quilting friends and students generously shared their lovely quilts (see the Galleries and pages 152-153 for credits). Connie, Jacque and Jan at the Kingston Quilt Shop were always enthusiastic and encouraging; I love teaching at their store. The book would not have been possible without the talents of Wanda Rains, whose beautiful machine quilting holds together 28 of the 48 quilts featured. Wanda's energy and friendship were a tremendous boost for maintaining the necessary momentum. My husband, Nigel, was especially helpful with computer issues and wonderful support throughout.

Table of Contents

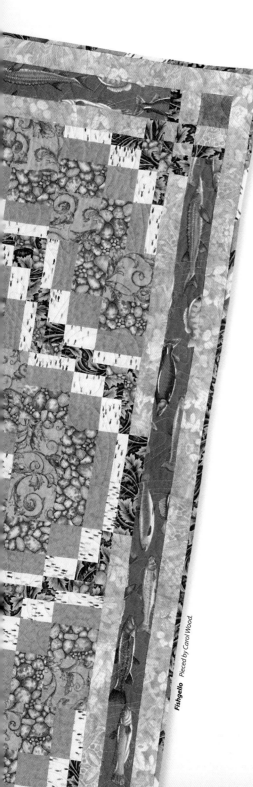

Fishgello *Pieced by Carol Wood.*

chapter 6

MORE AND MORE BLOCKS

chapter 7

ENLARGE THE BLOCK

Antigua *Pieced by Maggie Magee.*

Introduction

I learned the technique of making bargello quilts in 1991, when I took a class from quilter and fiber artist Alison Goss. I loved Alison's work and felt very inspired by the workshop. My first bargello quilt was symmetrical, but I gradually became more adventurous and enjoyed a freer approach, experimenting with increasing the complexity of the design and adding strip sets.

In the traditional bargello quilting method, named after a needlepoint technique, multiple strips of the same width (usually eight to ten strips, or sometimes as many as 20) are sewn together, then counter-cut in a variety of widths. The width size increases in specific increments; the strips are set adjacent and offset by one fabric. This creates the illusion of flowing curved lines, even though there is no curved piecing involved.

Many quilters find the large numbers of strips difficult to handle and are deterred from attempting these types of quilts. I have created a block in which only four strips are joined at a time so that the construction is much simpler. In addition, it is easy to generate a great variety of patterns by manipulating the block orientation. This technique draws on the principles of bargello quilting, using strip piecing and the same specific width increases in the strips and counter-cuts to create the flowing lines. Therefore, I've named it the Bargello block.

All the quilts in this book are made from the new Bargello block. I stumbled upon the idea quite by chance when I was looking through unusual settings for quilts on my computer in an The Electric Quilt Company® program. What I found was actually the mega-block used in Rebel (below and on page 118).

Rather than using it for a quilt setting, I drew it out as a 64-piece block and began to play with different arrangements. I then realized that if I divided it into four, I had a much more manageable 16-piece block that was easy to construct and remarkably versatile as well.

I was amazed by the number of attractive quilt patterns I could create from this one Bargello block. So began the series of quilts featured here. I taught the technique and was delighted by the excitement of my students.

My hope is that you, too, will enjoy exploring the many possibilities of this new Bargello block—and be inspired as well.

Rebel *Pieced by the author, machine quilted by Wanda Rains.*

The North Cascades Are Burning *Designed and made by the author in the traditional bargello method in 1994, a bad year for forest fires in the North Cascades around Mount Baker and Lake Chelan, Washington (43" × 48½"). Photo by Mark Frey.*

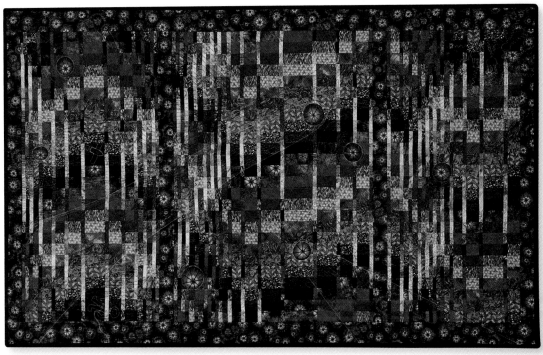

Galactic Autumn *Designed and made by the author in the traditional bargello method, 2001 (45" × 73"). Photo by Mark Frey.*

A Good Starter Project   *Bainbridge Delft (project quilt, page 92) is made from only one block type in a simple on-point setting.*

Options for Fabric Placement   *There are a multitude of options for fabric placement in the Bargello block; for example, the blue florals and white in this block from Bainbridge Delft.*

Options for Creative Quilting   *Bargello block quilts provide an opportunity for interesting quilting designs, as seen in this detail from Mississippi Sunflowers (project quilt, page 136). Photo by Mark Frey.*

Options for Increased Complexity   *Detail from Rebel, the author's first Bargello block quilt (project quilt, page 118) showing the original 64-piece mega-block, made from a cluster of four 16-piece blocks. Photo by Mark Frey.*

Bargello with a Twist of Orange Pieced by Gladys Schulz.

How to Use This Book

The Bargello block concept is new and unique. Here are some points to keep in mind:

- **Chapter One** contains useful basic guidelines for making your quilt, from fabric selection to attaching the binding.
- Study **Chapter Two** carefully before attempting the projects. Make sure that you fully understand how to plan the fabric placement and construct the block.
- Always read through all the directions for a project before you begin.
- The directions assume that you use a consistent ¼" seam allowance.
- A "full-width" strip is cut across the entire width of the fabric, selvage to selvage (40-42" depending on the fabric).
- A metric cutting table for 7" and 9½" blocks is provided in Appendix 4, page 147.

The projects are grouped in chapters by size and format:

Chapter Three – Small Quilts and Projects

Chapter Four – 36-Block Quilts (blocks set squarely; medium size, in the 50-55" range)

Chapter Five – Bargello Blocks on Point (medium size, in the 50-55" range)

Chapter Six – More and More Blocks (larger quilts, over 65")

Chapter Seven – Enlarge the Block (9½" blocks to make bed quilts)

The projects show you some of the many options for arranging the blocks. You may modify them in any way, using them as a starting point to make your creative juices flow. Each chapter includes a Gallery of unique Bargello block quilts made by my students.

The given fabric requirements for project quilts are generous to allow for errors. Adjust the fabric quantities if you decide to make additional blocks or change the number of fabrics.

"Block type" refers to particular fabric combinations in a block, so a quilt made from two block types has two sets of blocks, each with differing fabrics. The block pattern remains the same throughout; only the fabrics change.

In general, the quilts are easy to piece as long as you stay well organized when cutting all the strips. The most challenging aspects are determining which fabric goes where in the block and itemizing them in your cutting plan. I've done that part for you if you choose to use fabrics similar to those shown in the project quilts.

I encourage you to substitute your own fabric choices. Photocopy and use the block diagrams and cutting plan in the Appendices. You will also find two line drawings of project quilts to copy and color for planning your projects.

Have fun and enjoy your projects!

chapter 1

QUILTING BASICS

Before introducing you to the Bargello block, let's review the basics of quilting. If you're a new or inexperienced quilter, you will find this chapter to be a useful reference. More seasoned quilters may learn something, too!

I've provided advice on estimating fabric for your project, step-by-step instructions for accurately cutting strips and the basics of assembly line piecing. There's also a general supplies list so you can make sure you have everything you need to get started.

You'll learn how to create a backing for your quilt, and helpful tips will make it easier to select batting. Steps for basting, quilting and binding your quilt are covered in detail, leading to the triumphant conclusion: the labeling and hanging of your quilt!

Fabric Choices

Choose fabrics that you like, but try to include a wide variety of colors, values and print size—all important points to consider. Your choice will personalize your quilt and make it unique. If you don't know where to begin, try choosing a multicolored print (which could be a theme print), then pick out the matching colors in a variety of values.

You don't have to make all your choices before you begin. Often, I make my quilt blocks or the center of a quilt before deciding which fabrics to use in the setting and borders. Then, I audition different fabrics to see which ones I like the best. You may take your blocks to a store to test them with a variety of fabrics. There will be no shortage of people around to offer their opinions and assistance; but ultimately, the choice is yours.

FABRIC TIPS TO KEEP IN MIND

Quilters usually use 100 percent cotton fabrics and wash them before sewing.

On some fabrics, especially solid colors and batiks, it's hard to tell the right side from the back. If you can't tell, don't worry about it! There is no reason why you shouldn't use the back of a fabric as the "right" side if desired.

If you run out of a fabric, you may have to improvise with other fabrics or include extra pieced sections. Sometimes this can lead you along a more creative path—not always a bad thing!

Some quilters include different kinds of fabric in their quilts and add embellishments to create extra pizzazz or a variety of textures.

Explore Your Fabric Options   Be adventurous in your fabric choices, and don't be afraid to experiment and expand your horizons.

KEEP A RECORD

Record your fabric choices and cutting plan using the form provided (see Appendix 3, page 146) or in your own notebook.

Estimating Yardage

To estimate yardage, work out how many pieces of the required size will fit across one width of fabric (standard fabric width is 40-42"). Calculate the number of strips you will need to cut, and hence the total length of fabric needed. Allow yourself some extra in case of errors.

Border strips require long pieces of fabric unless you plan to piece them (see Adding Borders, page 48).

Quilt backs may need two or more full lengths of fabric if the quilt is wider than 40". Backs may be pieced from project leftovers or made from wider fabric (see page 20).

To calculate the amount of fabric needed for binding, measure the perimeter of the quilt and work out how many full-width 2½" strips to cut. If you have trouble making estimates, quilt store staff should be able to assist. Don't be afraid to ask for help if you need it.

GENERAL SUPPLIES

It takes more than fabric to make a quilt. Here is a list of useful quilting tools and supplies for the projects in this book.

- Sewing machine in good working order
- Iron and ironing board
- 45mm or 60mm rotary cutter
- 17" × 23" cutting mat, minimum size
- 6" × 24" quilters' ruler
- 6" × 12" quilters' ruler
- 15" × 15" square ruler
- Sewing scissors
- Small sticky labels
- Locking plastic bags for storage
- Mechanical pencil with fine lead (0.5mm)
- Colored pencils
- Batting
- Needles and pins
- Thread
- Decorative threads
- Sleeve roll
- Old dessert spoon
- Marking pencils or chalk pencils
- T-pins for basting
- Safety pins
- Seam ripper
- Masking tape
- Quilting computer software for designing
- Design work wall

DESIGN WORK WALL

Make a temporary work wall from a piece of batting or the back side of a vinyl tablecloth. Simply tape it to the wall while you're designing or laying out blocks.

Cutting Fabric

Accurate cutting will make all the difference in the ease with which you can sew the pieces together.

Taking the time to use rulers carefully and cut precisely is time well spent. Your cuts should be clean. If there are any irregular edges, straighten them up before cutting your next strip or patchwork piece.

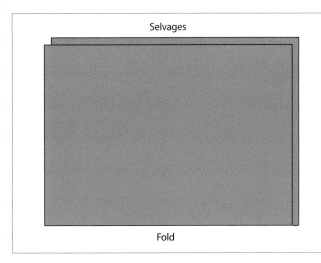

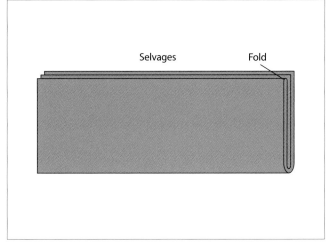

1. Press the fabric and fold selvage to selvage. You may find that the raw edge has not been cut straight, but make the fold so that the fabric will lie flat.

2. Fold the fabric again in the same direction. Place it flat on the cutting mat with the selvage edges at the top. You now have 4 layers of fabric.

CUTTING SIZES

To cut pieces wider than 6", use a large square ruler or measure from the grid of the cutting mat. Don't forget to cut your pieces large enough to include the ¼" seam allowance on each side. For example, a 1" × 7" sashing strip should be cut 1½" × 7½" to allow for the ¼" on each side.

ABOUT ROTARY CUTTERS

Rotary cutters are wonderful timesaving cutting tools. I recommend 45mm or 60mm rotary cutters with cutting mats sized 17" × 23" minimum and grided quilting rulers (such as Omnigrid®). Most of the time I use the 6" × 24" ruler. The 6" × 12" ruler is helpful for counter-cutting the strip sets for the Bargello block and the 15" square ruler for cutting setting blocks and triangles.

Never allow the rotary cutter to leave your hand with the blade exposed. I cannot emphasize this enough. Make a habit of closing the blade before you put it down (who knows, you may be interrupted), or use the type of cutter that automatically retracts its blade.

When you cannot easily cut through four layers of fabric, it's time for a new blade.

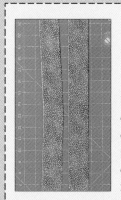

3. To make a cut to straighten the raw edge, line up a horizontal line on your 6" × 24" ruler with the fold at the bottom of the fabric. Move the ruler as close as possible to the raw edge of the fabric so there is a minimum of waste, but so that the raw edges on all of the layers of fabric are exposed.

Hold the ruler firmly in position with one hand. Hold the cutter as you would a sharp knife, with your forefinger extended and the shaft upright, with the blade flush against the ruler. Apply downward pressure and make the cut in one motion, moving the cutter away from yourself while keeping the blade next to the edge of the ruler.

Leave the ruler in place as you remove the excess fabric. If the cut did not penetrate all the layers, you can repeat the cut with the ruler still in place.

GO WITH THE GRAIN

When cutting fabric, pay attention to the direction of the grain. Grain is the way in which the fabric is woven.

The term "straight-of-grain" refers to both the lengthwise and cross grains of the fabric. Bias edges stretch and easily become misshapen, so patchwork pieces are usually cut with as many sides as possible aligned with the straight-of-grain.

Cut strips, squares and rectangles in alignment with the grain unless they are being fussy-cut for a particular motif in the fabric. Right-angled triangles will have at least one bias edge. If the long side of a setting triangle is on the outer edge of the quilt, cut the triangle so that the long edge is on the straight-of-grain, making the two short sides on the bias. Do not use the selvages.

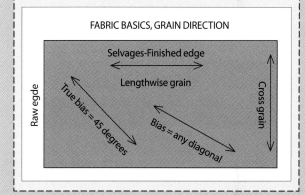

FABRIC BASICS, GRAIN DIRECTION

Selvages-Finished edge

Lengthwise grain

Raw edge

Cross grain

True bias = 45 degrees

Bias = any diagonal

4. Carefully rotate the fabric without disturbing the straight edge, or move around the table to the other side of the cutting board. Cut strips the desired width, using a ruler.

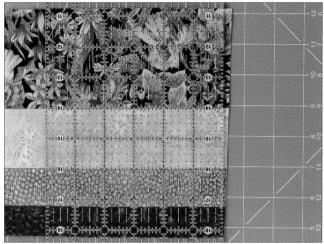

5. In the Bargello block technique, strip sets of 4 full-width strips are joined and counter-cut into segments of the desired size. To make the counter-cuts, repeat Step 3 to remove the selvages and straighten the edge (line up a horizontal line on the ruler with one of the seam lines).

7. Make sure the raw edge remains vertical. As you make repeated counter-cuts, your raw edge may become slightly skewed. Check it periodically (for example, after each 4 or 5 cuts) by placing the ruler over the remaining strip set and lining up horizontal lines on the ruler with the seam lines. If the raw edge is no longer completely vertical, repeat Step 3 to correct and straighten it.

6. Repeat Step 4. Counter-cut the strip sets into segments of the desired width.

Assembly Line Piecing

Assembly line piecing saves time and thread. It enables you to sew edge to edge from piece to piece without interruption. You can machine piece several units of fabric together one after another in a long chain without lifting the presser foot or cutting the threads between the units.

Being consistent and precise will make piecing much easier. Plan the order in which you assemble the pieces so that you always sew in straight lines, avoiding insetting corners. All the quilts in this book can be pieced without any insetting, and backstitching is used only when mitering the corners on borders.

Always use a ¼" seam allowance when sewing patchwork pieces together. Use a ¼" foot on your machine, or adjust the position of the needle to make the accurate allowance.

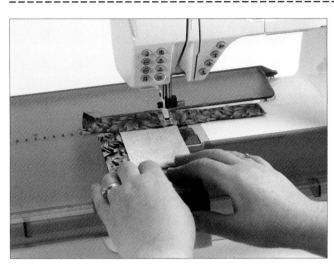

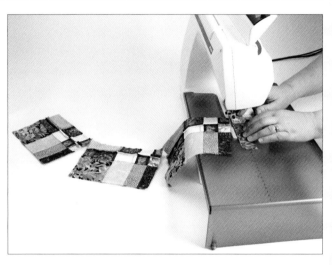

1. Start by sewing on a small scrap of fabric folded in half. I call this scrap the spacer strip.

Lay or pin the first patchwork pieces together and feed into the machine. Allow the machine to continue sewing a stitch or two after it passes the edge of the fabric.

2. Feed the next patchwork pieces into the machine, continuing in a chain. By adding a spacer strip at the end of each batch, you'll always be ready to start sewing again without lifting the presser foot.

FINISHED AND UNFINISHED SIZES

"Finished size" is the measurement of a completed piece, block or quilt top not including the ¼" seam allowance. So, a 7" or 9½" quilt block is the finished size.

"Unfinished size" is the measurement of an uncompleted piece, block or quilt top, raw edge to raw edge, unassembled, including the ¼" seam allowance all around. Therefore, an unfinished 7½" block measures 7" finished; an unfinished 10" block measures 9½" finished.

Quilt Backs and Batting

When the quilt top is completed, it should be layered with batting and a backing. Again, there are choices to be made, which will significantly affect the outcome.

Backing Your Quilt

Quilt backs for small quilts are easy. Simply cut the back a little larger than the quilt, to at least 1½" on each side. Allow this extra margin of fabric on all quilt backs in case of fabric uptake or distortion during quilting. Any excess is trimmed later.

For quilts larger than 40" wide, the quilt back must be pieced, unless you purchase wider fabric. Many quilting stores have a small selection of wide fabrics that make excellent quilt backs. This is an economical way to buy the fabric and avoids the necessity for seams.

Use your fabric efficiently by planning carefully. Long cuts of fabric are needed for border strips on the quilt top; the leftovers may be used to piece the quilt back, along with other leftover fabrics from the top. Remember that the more pieces you use, the more seam allowances there will be when quilting.

Choosing Batting

There are many types of batting available, and choosing the appropriate one may be a little daunting. Read the packaging carefully for the batting content, the height of the loft and how far apart you can stitch the lines of quilting.

Batting of 100 percent cotton is warm, but usually requires a higher density of quilting than polyester. A blend of 80 percent cotton and 20 percent polyester is often a good compromise

because the polyester bonds the cotton, so quilting lines may be farther apart.

Some cotton batting contains a scrim, a very thin mesh of plastic to hold the cotton together. This type of batting works well for wall hangings.

I like to use low or medium loft batting. However, if you want a poofy look, go for the high loft batting. Polyester tends to be poofier than cotton.

Wool and silk battings are also available. Some types of batting shrink when they are washed. Check the directions on the packaging to see if the batting needs prewashing.

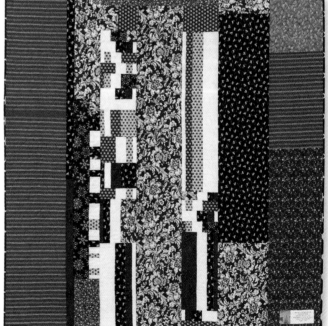

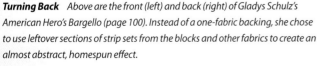

Turning Back *Above are the front (left) and back (right) of Gladys Schulz's American Hero's Bargello (page 100). Instead of a one-fabric backing, she chose to use leftover sections of strip sets from the blocks and other fabrics to create an almost abstract, homespun effect.*

Basting

Basting stitches temporarily hold the three layers of the quilt together during quilting. They are removed once the quilting is completed. Baste with long running stitches in a grid, or use safety pins or a basting gun with plastic tacks. Spray-on adhesives and iron-on battings are also available. I prefer traditional basting stitches.

A Simple Tool for Easier Basting *A spoon makes an excellent tool for lifting the needle from the quilt surface.*

1. Press the top and back of the quilt. The seams on the quilt back may be pressed open.

2. Lay the quilt back flat, wrong side up. Use a table (one that has a nonscratch surface or that you don't mind scratching), hard floor or low-pile carpet. I use a table for small quilts and baste large quilts on the floor.

3. Secure the quilt back. Tape the quilt back to the surface with masking tape, or use T-pins on a carpet. Secure the opposing sides, working from the center out to the corners. Repeat for the other two sides. Make sure the quilt back is perfectly flat. It should be taut but not stretched to the point of distortion.

4. Add the middle of the sandwich by placing the batting on top of the backing. Gently smooth it so there are no wrinkles.

5. Place the quilt top, right side up, over the batting. Make sure the top is positioned centrally over the quilt back and that there is at least a 1½" margin of quilt back and batting exposed around each edge of the top. Check that it is perfectly flat and square. Straight seams sometimes appear a little crooked; gently manipulate the quilt top to align them correctly.

6. Secure the quilt top. If you are working on a carpet, T-pin the quilt top as you did the back. On a table, put safety pins in the corners and the center of each side through all three layers.

7. Baste the quilt using quilting or regular thread, a large needle, and a spoon to lift the needle from the surface of the quilt. Baste a grid of long running stitches all over the quilt. Start in the middle of one side of the quilt and baste all the way across. You may knot the thread or make a couple of backstitches to start.

Take 4 or 5 stitches before pulling the thread all the way through. This saves time, especially if your thread is long. The second line of basting stitches should be about a hand's width away from the first.

Continue basting the lines until you are near the edges of the quilt, then baste at right angles, creating a grid.

8. Remove the tape or pins from the edges of the quilt. Baste ½" to 1" from the edges all the way around.

9. Quilt the sandwich. Remove the basting stitches except for those around the perimeter of the quilt. These are taken out after the binding is attached.

Quilting

The quilting stitches are a vital component since they hold the three layers of the quilting sandwich together. Also, they may greatly enhance the appearance of the quilt. Quilting stitch patterns show up particularly well on solid colors or pale monochromatic fabrics and small prints.

Quilting stitches may be sewn by machine (commercially or on a regular home sewing machine) or by hand. Whatever the method, the stitches should be of an even density.

As with piecing, there are numerous options for quilting stitches. In Bargello block quilts, the patterns are usually pretty busy, so the quilts lend themselves well to overall quilting designs. If you have plain setting blocks between the Bargello blocks, you have an opportunity for fancier quilting that will be more visible.

There are many instructional books and videos available for further information on hand- and machine- quilting techniques.

Machine Quilting

When machine quilting, I like to stabilize the quilt, usually by quilting in the ditch along the seams between the blocks before quilting inside the blocks. Quilting accurately in the ditch can be challenging, so I often use a serpentine stitch along the seams or in a diagonal grid. (See the detail from Mayan Mystery in the photo below.)

The serpentine stitch is very forgiving and looks attractive, especially in variegated rayon threads. Change the machine needle to a topstitch size 90 when using fancy threads. Use a walking foot for straight-line stitching. Drop your feed dogs and use a darning foot for free-motion quilting.

Long-Arm Quilting

Since I don't enjoy manhandling the bulk of a large quilt in a regular sewing machine, I usually give my big quilts (over about 50" square) to my friend Wanda Rains for quilting on her long-arm machine. Commercial quilters offer a wide range of pattern options, from allover pantographs to custom designs. Discuss the possibilities with your quilter.

The Serpentine Stitch *The serpentine stitch reliably stabilizes the quilt. It looks attractive and does not interfere with the complexities of a Bargello pattern. Detail from Mayan Mystery (project quilt, page 70.)*

MACHINE MAINTENANCE

Keep your sewing machine in good working order.
Clear out the lint frequently, and take it to your dealer
for annual cleaning and maintenance checkups.

Detail of Mississippi Sunflowers *This detail of Mississippi Sunflowers (project quilt, page 136) shows the beautiful pattern quilted by Wanda Rains. The stylized designs you can accomplish will add a new level of artistry to your Bargello quilt. Photo by Mark Frey.*

QUILTING SHRINKS THE QUILT

The action of quilting may contract the quilt top as
much as 1–2" on a large quilt.

Binding

Binding strips may be cut on the straight-of-grain of the fabric unless the quilt has curved or irregular edges.

I recommend a French (double) binding since it is strong and durable and finishes the quilt with a firm edge.

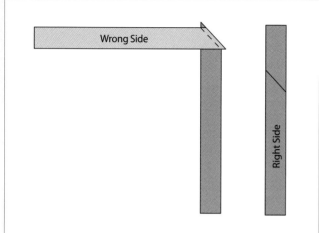

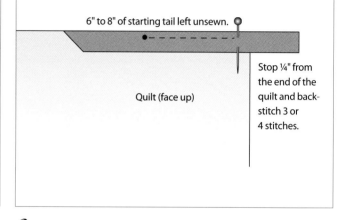

1. Begin by calculating the number of binding strips needed. For fabric 42" wide, measure the perimeter of the quilt and divide by 40. Option: If the binding fabric is the same as the border strips that were cut lengthwise, you also may cut the binding strips lengthwise from the leftover piece. This creates longer strips and reduces the number of seams.

Cut 2½"-wide binding strips. Cut the ends of the strips at 45-degree angles and join them together. Press the seams open and press the binding in half lengthwise with the wrong sides together.

2. Begin to attach the binding to the quilt. The quilt should be quilted but still have those basting stitches that are ½" to 1" from the outer edge.

Align the raw edge of the binding with the raw edge of the quilt top. Start stitching about 10" below a corner, leaving a tail of 6-8" of binding to join at the end. Preferably, use a walking foot on your machine.

Stop ¼" from the first corner, make 3 or 4 back-stitches and remove the quilt from the sewing machine.

NEEDLE REPLACEMENT

Replace the needle in your sewing machine after about 10 hours of sewing.

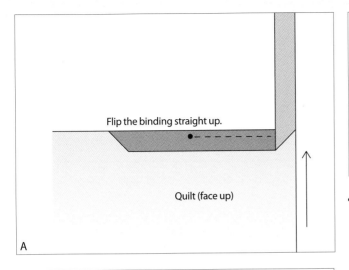

Flip the binding straight up.

Quilt (face up)

A

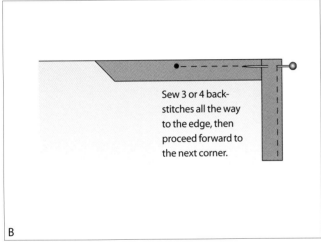

Sew 3 or 4 back-stitches all the way to the edge, then proceed forward to the next corner.

B

3. To turn the corner, rotate the quilt a quarter turn. Fold the binding straight up, away from the corner, making a 45-degree angle fold (A). Bring the binding straight down in line with the next raw edge to be sewn (B).

The top fold of the binding should be even with the edge just sewn.

4. Continue sewing the binding to the quilt top, backstitching to the edge of the top fold, then stitching until you reach ¼" from the next corner. Stop and backstitch. Continue this way for all sides of the quilt.

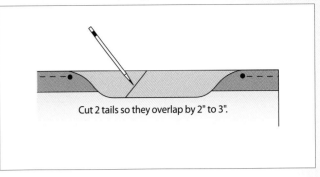

Cut 2 tails so they overlap by 2" to 3".

5. To join the binding ends, fold the binding at the corner as previously described in Step 3; pin it by the top fold. Trim the end of the binding to join it with a 45-degree angle seam to the 6-8" tail you left at the start.

Open the binding ends. Draw a pencil line at 45 degrees where they join.

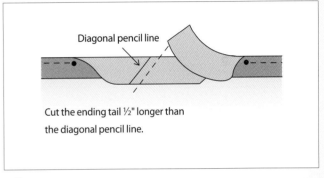

Diagonal pencil line

Cut the ending tail ½" longer than the diagonal pencil line.

6. Cut the tail ½" away from the pencil line to accommodate the seam allowance. Stitch the binding ends together and finger press the seam open.

7. To finish sewing the binding, begin with backstitches at the corner and continue until you meet the starting point. Remove the basting stitches. Use a rotary cutter or scissors to trim excess batting and backing flush with the quilt top and binding raw edge. Your binding should be stuffed evenly with batting, so trim carefully.

8. Bring the folded edge of the binding to the back of the quilt, covering the machine stitching line. Hand-stitch the binding down with a blind stitch (match the thread color to the binding, not the quilt back). Miter the corners by folding over the unstitched binding from the next edge to form a 45-degree angle.

As an alternative, machine sew the binding to the back of the quilt first, then bring the binding to the front, top-stitching with a zigzag or decorative stitch.

Labeling Your Quilt

Years from now, people will be curious about the creation of your quilt: who made it, when and where. Include a label on your quilt showing that information. The label may be embroidered, printed by hand using a permanent fabric marker or computer-generated. If you use markers to make the label by hand, first iron freezer paper to the back of the fabric to stabilize it while you're writing.

Appliqué your label to the back of the quilt. I usually position the label in a lower corner; it can be seen easily by lifting the corner when the quilt is hanging.

Savannah Sunrise

Bargello Quilts with a Twist
On-pointer with sashing
Designed and pieced by Maggie Ball
Machine quilted by Wanda Rains
Summer 2007

Maggie Ball
Bainbridge Island, WA

Computer-Generated Label   *This label is printed on specially treated paper-backed fabric for use with an inkjet printer.*

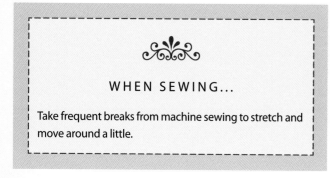

WHEN SEWING...

Take frequent breaks from machine sewing to stretch and move around a little.

Hanging Your Quilt

To display your quilt as a wall hanging, make a sleeve to attach to the back along the top edge. The sleeve is a fabric tube wide enough to accommodate a dowel, which may be positioned on hooks or suspended by fishing line from museum-style hangers on the wall.

This method eliminates any bulging on the front of the quilt around the dowel. Use plain muslin or a fabric that matches the quilt back.

---

1. Cut a strip for the sleeve. For a sleeve 4" wide, cut a fabric strip 8½" wide and 2" shorter than the quilt top.

2. Turn and hem. On each short end, turn under ¼" twice. Machine stitch using a straight stitch close to the hem fold.

3. Fold the sleeve in half lengthwise with right sides together. Machine stitch ¼" from the raw edges; backstitch to start and end the seam. Turn right side out and press.

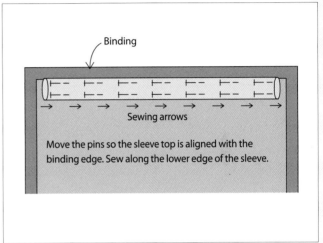

Binding

Sewing arrows

Move the pins so the sleeve top is aligned with the binding edge. Sew along the lower edge of the sleeve.

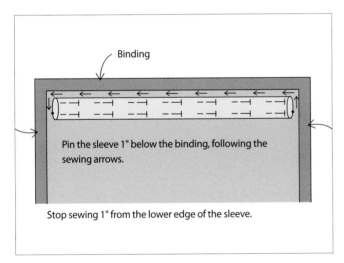

Binding

Pin the sleeve 1" below the binding, following the sewing arrows.

Stop sewing 1" from the lower edge of the sleeve.

5. Reposition the fold in the sleeve as well as the pins.
   Move the sleeve up so that the top fold is just below the binding and pin it in place. Blind stitch along the bottom edge of the sleeve. Remove the pins.
   Hang the quilt and enjoy!

4. Pin the sleeve to the quilt along the top edge, 1" below the binding.
   Blind stitch the sleeve to the quilt back, taking care that your stitches don't pass all the way through to show on the front. Start 1" from the lower edge of one end of the sleeve, stitch across the top and down the other edge, stopping 1" from the bottom. The sleeve is now sewn on three sides.

chapter 2

MAKING THE BARGELLO BLOCK

The construction of the Bargello block involves the simple strip piecing of four sets of four strips. These four strip sets are then counter-cut into segments; one of each segment is joined to complete the 16-piece block.

The challenge is to stay well organized throughout, so that the strips and segments remain in the correct order during the piecing and block assembly. Read this chapter thoroughly and make sure that you fully understand the technique before diving in. If you follow the steps carefully, you should find the process straightforward and easy to master. Copy and use the blank block diagrams and cutting plan in Appendices 1-3 (pages 144-146). Refer to Appendices 5 and 6 (pages 148-149) for an additional example of a completed diagram and cutting plan. Appendix 4 (page 147) provides quilter-friendly metric conversions.

Once you have become proficient at this technique, you may find it rather addictive! There are so many creative ways to play with the blocks and to generate new patterns. Of course, your personalized fabric choices make every quilt unique, even if you choose to replicate one of the projects in subsequent chapters.

The Bargello Block Pattern

The Bargello block is composed of 16 patches. The four squares along the diagonal gradually decrease in size. **A1** is the largest in the top left, followed by **B2**, then **C3**, and the smallest in the lower right, **D4**. The other pieces are all rectangles arranged symmetrically around this diagonal; one side is the mirror image of the other. The block is divided into four segments, called the **A**, **B**, **C** and **D** segments. Each segment is created by counter-cutting the **A**, **B**, **C** and **D** strip sets.

The **A**, **B**, **C** and **D** strip sets are made by strip piecing four full-width strips of fabric (cut selvage to selvage, 40-42"). Strip piecing is the technique in which strips of fabric are cut and joined length-wise. Each strip set is made of four strips that decrease in width, all the **1**s being the widest and the **4**s being the narrowest.

When the strip sets are completed, they are counter-cut to create the **A**, **B**, **C** and **D** segments. The **A** set is counter-cut the widest, the **B** narrower, the **C** narrower still and the **D** narrowest. The **A**, **B**, **C** and **D** segments are joined to complete the block.

All of the projects in this book are made from 7" blocks except for those in Chapter Seven – *Enlarge the Block*. That chapter features the 9½" block.

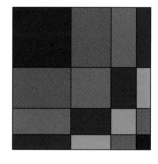

A1	B1	C1	D1
A2	B2	C2	D2
A3	B3	C3	D3
A4	B4	C4	D4

Bargello Block Diagram Showing Components

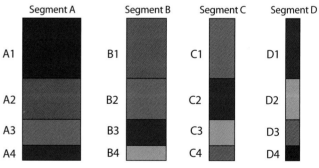

Completed Block with Component Segments Labels illustrate the placement of patchwork pieces and the **A**, **B**, **C** and **D** segments.

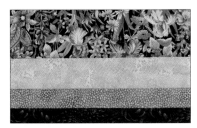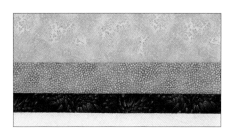

The A Strip Set *contains full-width strips of fabrics for the **A1**, **A2**, **A3** and **A4** pieces.*

The B Strip Set *contains full-width strips of fabrics for the **B1**, **B2**, **B3** and **B4** pieces.*

A strip set	B strip set	C strip set	D strip set

The Completed Bargello Block *The strip segments are joined to form the Bargello block. Compare this finished block with the diagram on the opposite page.*

The C Strip Set *contains full-width strips of fabrics for the **C1**, **C2**, **C3** and **C4** pieces.*

The D Strip Set *contains full-width strips of fabrics for the **D1**, **D2**, **D3**, and **D4** pieces.*

Determining Your Fabrics

The project patterns include block diagrams and full instructions, so the fabric placement has already been determined for you. Feel free to make substitutions. If you would like to design your own block, use the guidelines that follow.

How Many Fabrics?

Use as few as two fabrics or as many as nine in the Bargello block. In most of the project quilts, the blocks contain between four and seven fabrics.

Using only two fabrics will produce a checkerboard effect. Nine fabrics become rather complex and busy. It is important to choose a wide range of values from dark to light so that the emerging patterns stand out. Also, try to include fabrics with a variety of print scales and textures to add interest.

Choosing Colors

Value is more important than color, but you should choose colors that you like. Avoid an entirely monochromatic selection unless you add black or white.

Try to include a zinger fabric; for example, a color from the other side of the color wheel that will pop out. Adding black will help ntensify your colors. White will have the opposite effect, softening the look.

If you don't know where to begin, choose a multicolored theme print and add fabrics that go with it, remembering to include lights, mediums and darks.

Creativity and Challenge   *Select a variety of values and print scales in your fabric choices to make your own unique Bargello blocks.*

Gothic Medallion   *This project quilt (page 94) pulls colors from the theme print (below).*

Using a Multicolored Theme Print   *This fabric, used in Gothic Medallion (above), suggests a range of fabric color choices.*

WHAT IS A BLOCK TYPE?

The term "block type" refers to particular fabric combinations in a block. A quilt made from two block types has two sets of blocks each with differing fabrics. The block pattern remains the same throughout.

Arranging Fabric

Arrange the fabrics symmetrically around the diagonal line of squares in the block so that each side of the line is a mirror image of the other. There are several possibilities. You may place the same fabric in all the squares along the diagonal or have a different one in each square. Alternatively, configure them in concentric arcs around the large **A1** square. The illustrations below depict these options.

The arc **A4-B3-C2-D1** is particularly important in helping to create secondary patterns when the blocks are assembled. My recommendation is to place a very light or a very dark fabric in this arc. Make the arcs on either side (**A3-B2-C1** and **B4-C3-D2**) highly contrast that choice.

Another key choice is the fabric for the **A1** piece, which is large—3" in the 7" block. In some configurations, four of these **A1** squares come together to create a 6" square, so it's important to consider how they will look.

You may find it helpful to look at the projects in this book to see how the fabrics are arranged in the blocks. I advise using one of the book projects for your first attempt, making direct fabric-for-fabric substitutions. This will give you a better idea of the whole process, and the versatility of the block, before you begin designing on your own.

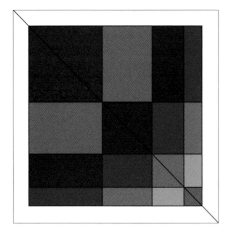

Arcs *Fabrics are arranged in concentric arcs around the **A1**.*

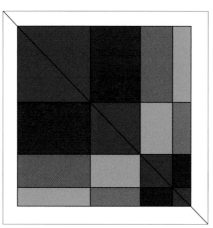

Diagonal Line *All the squares on the diagonal are the same fabric.*

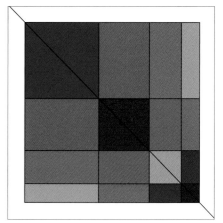

Variety *All the squares on the diagonal are a different fabric.*

A1	B1	C1	D1
A2	B2	C2	D2
A3	B3	C3	D3
A4	B4	C4	D4

The A4-B3-C2-D1 Arc
This arc tends to play an important visual role in the overall pattern. Choose fabrics carefully. Very light or very dark fabrics work well with highly contrasting fabrics on either side.

Chasing Butterflies *The turquoise in the **A4**-**B3**-**C2**-**D1** arcs outlines the butterfly shapes in this tessellated butterflies layout. The small black **C4**-**D3** arcs also pop (Gallery quilt, page 64).*

Deck of Pansies *The secondary patterns of colored circles are produced by the **A4**-**B3**-**C2**-**D1** arcs (project quilt, page 74).*

Irregular Furrows *Fabric choices and positioning of all **A1** fabrics in this Gallery quilt (page 86) were made at the layout stage on the work wall.*

NEED METRIC CONVERSIONS FOR THE BARGELLO BLOCK?

You'll find a handy metric conversion chart for the 7" and 9½" Bargello blocks in Appendix 4 on page 147.

Layout Options

Look at the variety of patterns that may be generated from only 16 blocks. If the number of blocks is increased, the possibilities become even more numerous.

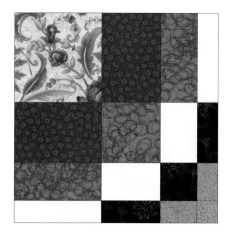

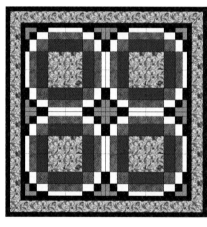

Your Fabric Cutting Plan

Once you have determined your fabric arrangement, create a block diagram, using a copy of Appendix 1 or 2 (pages 144-145). Annotate the diagram with your fabric choices. You can use colored pencils or written notes; or you can cut and stick a snip of the appropriate fabric to the diagram. The goal is to easily recognize which fabric goes where.

Once you've completed your annotated block diagram, transfer the information to a fabric cutting plan. This plan lists each fabric in turn and itemizes the sizes and quantities of

the full-width strips required. Use the cutting plan, rather than the block diagram, as a guide when you cut your strips, systematically cutting all the strips from each particular fabric in turn. The block diagram includes the cutting sizes of all the strips.

Let's assume that we want to make sixteen 7" blocks from full-width strips. The counter-cut **A** segments will be 3½" wide. In order to cut 16 segments, you will need two **A** strip sets; therefore, two full-width strips of each of the **A1**, **A2**, **A3** and **A4** fabrics are required.

Photocopy and use the blank cutting plan form found in Appendix 3 (page 146). Using your annotated block diagram, list the fabrics in turn with the strip measurements. The strip widths are noted on the diagram. Notice that all the **1**s (**A1**, **B1**, **C1** and **D1**) are 3½", all the **2**s are 2½", all the **3**s are 1¾" and all the **4**s are 1¼". Use full-width strips of fabric cut selvage to selvage (40-42"); or, for fat quarters, double the numbers of strips. Here's an example from Rambling Roses (page 63).

Bargello Block Diagram

A1	B1	C1	D1
A2	B2	C2	D2
A3	B3	C3	D3
A4	B4	C4	D4

Fabric Cutting Plan

Fabric (describe) _Flowers_
| Set A A1 – 3½" x 2 | Set C C3 – 1¾" |
| Set B B2 – 2½" | Set D D4 – 1¼" |

Fabric _Blue_
| Set A A2 – 2½" x 2 | Set C |
| Set B B1 – 3½" | Set D |

Fabric _Pink_
| Set A A3 – 1¾" x 2 | Set C C1 – 3½" |
| Set B B4 – 1¼" | Set D D2 – 2½" |

Fabric _Dark Blue_
| Set A A4 – 1¼" x 2 | Set C C2 – 2½", C4 – 1¼" |
| Set B B3 – 1¾" | Set D D1 – 3½", D3 – 1¾" |

Fabric _____
| Set A | Set C |
| Set B | Set D |

Fabric _____
| Set A | Set C |
| Set B | Set D |

1. Begin with the fabric in the top left-hand corner, the **A1** piece.

Write something to identify the particular fabric. In this case we will call it "Flowers." This flower fabric appears in 4 places in the block, so complete the cutting plan as follows, remembering that you need 2 sets of strips of all the **A**s to make the 16 blocks.

Set **A A1** – 3½" × 2
Set **B B2** – 2½"
Set **C C3** – 1¾"
Set **D D4** – 1¼"

2. Move down the **A** segment to the next fabric and do the same thing.

The fabric is "Blue." Note that the blue fabric does not appear in the **C** or **D** sets, so those entries will be blank.

Set **A A2** – 2½" × 2
Set **B B1** – 3½"
Set **C** [blank]
Set **D** [blank]

3. The next fabric in the **A** segment is "Pink."

Set **A A3** – 1¾" × 2
Set **B B4** – 1¼"
Set **C C1** – 3½"
Set **D D2** – 2½"

4. The last fabric in the **A** segment is "Dark Blue."

Note that the dark blue appears twice in the **C** and **D** sets, so they will each have two entries.

Set **A A4** – 1¼" × 2
Set **B B3** – 1¾"
Set **C C2** – 2½", **C4** – 1¼"
Set **D D1** – 3½", **D3** – 1¾"

LOOK IN THE APPENDICES

Appendices 1 and 2: 7" and 9½" blocks with cutting sizes of strips
Appendix 3: Blank cutting plan form to photocopy
Appendix 4: Metric measurements for Bargello blocks
Appendices 5 and 6: Full-size examples of the annotated block diagram and the completed cutting plan form

---

This particular block has only four different fabrics and all of them appear in the **A** segment. For a block with more fabrics, move to the **B** segment and repeat the the steps, and then to the **C** and **D** segments. Double-check the plan before you begin cutting. There are 16 pieces in the block, so you should have 16 entries on your plan.

Now you are ready to wield your rotary cutter and really get going! The most challenging part is over. Providing you stay well organized, the cutting and block construction will be a piece of cake.

CUTTING A1 SQUARES SEPARATELY

If you use a directional print or fussy-cut a motif, you can manipulate the orientation by cutting the squares separately (instead of strip piecing them with the other **A** set strips). In several quilts I did just that, cutting **A1** squares and the **A** segments from an **A2**, **A3**, **A4** strip set. If you piece the rest of the block, joining the **B**, **C** and **D** segments, you can arrange all these sections of blocks on a work wall and play with the **A1** squares.

You could consider using a variety of fabrics for the **A1**, or even make every **A1** square different. Determine the desired orientation of the **A1** piece, then complete the piecing of the block, being careful to remember the position of the block in the layout. I usually remove and sew them one at a time, placing them straight back on the work wall to avoid confusion.

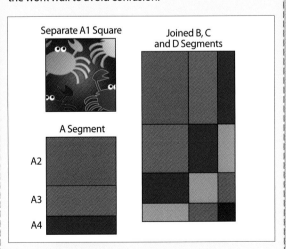

The Orientation of the A1 Square *Working with block sections in a layout provides the option of manipulating the position of the A1 square.*

Constructing Bargello Blocks

Practice the technique by starting with a small project (see Chapter Three). If you begin by piecing 16 blocks all the same, you can make a small quilt. Sew additional blocks later (maybe adding some different fabrics) for a larger and more complex quilt.

Use the cutting plan provided for the project you select, or make your own to design your own fabric configuration (see pages 38-39). For instructions on accurate rotary cutting and counter-cutting to make the segments, see Chapter One. Directions for pinning and press-ing follow in this chapter. Please read and pay careful attention to these.

The cutting plan lists each fabric with the widths of the strips and the quantity of strips. Here are the steps, using the 7" block as the example. For the enlarged 9½" block, see Chapter Seven.

| A | B | C | D |

 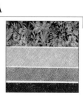 

1. Label 4 pieces of scrap paper **A**, **B**, **C** and **D**, 1 letter on each. Cut all the strips needed from each fabric in turn.

As you cut the strips, place them on the appropriate sheet so that all the As (**A1**, **A2**, **A3** and **A4**) are on the **A** sheet and so on. For 16 blocks, you will have 2 of each strip on the **A** sheet, and 1 of each strip on the other 3 sheets. Each strip set should contain 4 different-sized strips: 3½", 2½", 1¾" and 1¼".

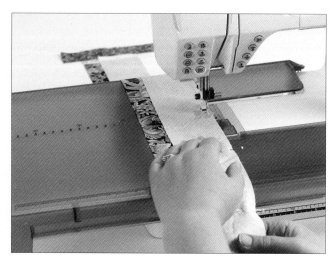

2. Piece each strip set in turn. Lay the 2½" strip on top of the 3½" strip (widest strip under the next-widest strip). Sew the strips together along the long edge. Repeat for the other 2 strips. (If you always place the smaller of the 2 strips in each pair on top, your strips will remain in the correct order.) Press the seams of the strip pairs open as directed on page 43.

❧ PIECING ODD SEGMENTS

Sometimes 12 blocks are required, but one **A** set yields only 11 segments.

Don't make another **A** strip set. Cut a 3½" segment from a **B** strip set. Rip seams and trim pieces to the correct size: **B1** becomes **A2** (3½" × 2½"), **B2** becomes **A3** (3½" × 1¾") and **B3** becomes **A4** (3½" × 1¼").

Cut the 3½" **A1** square separately. Assemble the pieces into an **A** segment for the twelfth block.

Likewise, to create an extra **B** segment, cut a 2½" segment from a **C** set; or for an extra **C** segment, cut a 1¾" segment from a **D** set.

Use the table below to plan the number of strip sets for your own designs.

YIELD OF SEGMENTS FROM FULL-WIDTH STRIP SETS FOR 7" BLOCKS			
Segment Sets	**One Set**	**Two Sets**	**Three Sets**
A (3½")	11	22	33
B (2½")	16	32	48
C (1¾")	22	44	66
D (1¼")	32	64	96

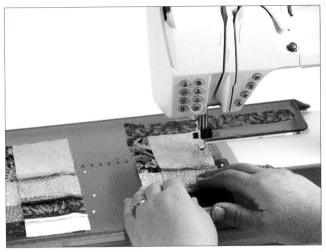

3. Sew the strip pairs together. Strips 1 and 2 (3½" and 2½") go on the bottom, strips 3 and 4 (the 1¾" and 1¼") on top so that the seam line joins 2 to 3 (the 2½" strip to the 1¾" strip). Press the seam open.

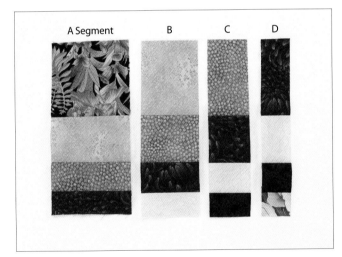

4. Counter-cut the strip sets to make the block segments. See page 18 for counter-cutting instructions. Make 16 counter-cuts from each strip set as follows:

     A Sets – 3½"
     B Set – 2½"
     C Set – 1¾"
     D Set – 1¼"
     You now have **A**, **B**, **C** and **D** segments.

5. Join the segments in pairs, just as you did with the strips. Always place the wider of the 2 on the bottom: **B** goes on top of **A**, **D** goes on top of **C**. Pin at the seam intersections. Always sew from the largest piece (number 1) to the smallest piece (number 4).

Press the seams open on the pairs of segments. You may find a sleeve roll helpful (see page 43).

6. Join the segment pairs. Once again place the smaller segments (**C** and **D**) on top of the larger segments (**A** and **B**) so that the seam joins **B** to **C**. Again, sew from the largest piece (number 1) to the smallest piece (number 4). Press the final seam open. The block is completed.

Pinning

Use pins when you feel the need to stabilize the pieces as you sew. Place them perpendicular to the sewing line with the heads extending ¼" to ½" beyond the raw edges so that they can be removed easily as you sew.

I always pin at the intersections of pieced sections. For the Bargello block, this means pinning at each intersection when joining the segments from strip sets **A**, **B**, **C** and **D** together. I also always pin when I sew bias edges and when adding long border strips.

If your cutting or piecing is inaccurate, sometimes you will need to ease in extra amounts of fabric when you join two pieces. This most commonly occurs when you attach long border strips to the center field of the quilt. Distribute the excess evenly along the length of the seam by pinning the ends and centers together first, then halfway between the center and the end, and so on. If the longer of the fabrics is placed on the underside when you stitch, it will be easier to accommodate the excess. For two pieced sections, pin all the seam intersections first to make sure they are in the correct position and then, if necessary, add more pins in between.

Pinning A and B, and C and D Before Stitching *Here sets **A** and **B** are pinned together, their seams pressed open and right sides of the fabric facing one another. Keep the smaller **B** set on top when you feed the pieces into the sewing machine. Sets **C** and **D** are also pinned together in the same manner.*

*Once these are sewn, lay the **C** and **D** piece over the **A** and **B** piece, pin so the intersections are aligned, and then sew.*

Top Side of the Finished Block

Wrong Side of the Finished Block *Shows the seams pressed open.*

Pressing

To press, use the iron on the hot cotton setting. I like to use steam. Usually, seam allowances are pressed to one side, towards the darkest fabric. However, for the Bargello block all the seams are pressed open because it is difficult to accurately predict which way to press so that seams on adjacent blocks will butt in opposite directions. When the blocks are assembled adjacently, those seams are also pressed open so that no bulky intersections arise.

Each Bargello strip set contains 4 strips. Sew the strips in pairs (see further details on pages 40-41), press the seams open, and join the pairs together and press that seam open. This is much easier than joining all 4 strips together and then trying to press all 3 seams open.

The same applies when sewing the strip set segments together to assemble the block.

1. Run the iron along the seam to set it before pressing it open.

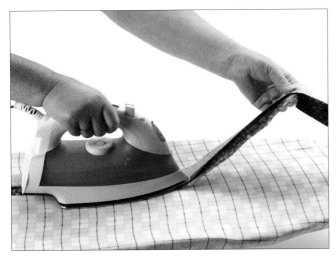

2. With the wrong side up, start opening the seam with your fingers, then continue with the tip of the iron. Hold the opposite end of the pair of strips raised as you iron (you'll have a harder time if you leave the strips lying flat on the ironing board).

3. When all strips of a set are sewn together, repeat Steps 1 and 2, then turn and press again from the top side. Iron along the seam line, gently pulling the fabric taut. If the seam looks bowed, pull tighter and iron again. Spray starch may be used at this stage.

4. When the segments are joined to create a block, press the seams open. A sleeve roll may be helpful.

Arranging Bargello Blocks

The way in which you arrange the blocks in your quilt top will dramatically affect the appearance. There are so many possibilities, and it is great fun to play around trying out a variety of configurations. I often make my blocks before I decide how to put them together. Then, when the blocks are completed, I audition different layouts.

If you have a digital camera, you can take photos of the various layouts to keep a record and make comparisons. Not only can you make several different patterns by setting the blocks adjacent, either squarely or on-point, but you can create a completely different look by adding sashing strips or even offsetting the blocks slightly.

If you have access to a computer program for designing quilts, such as EQ6 (The Electric Quilt Company®), draw the Bargello block and add it to your block library. You can easily experiment with an enormous variety of choices when designing your quilt.

Rotate the blocks, include additional block types with different fabrics, change the layout and add sashing strips. I designed most of the quilts in this book with the aid of my computer.

There are many more complex examples in the following project chapters of this book. I encourage you to experiment and create your own variations.

Here are some setting options:
- Blocks square and adjacent.
- Blocks with sashing strips in between, cornerstones optional.
- Blocks with pieced sashing strips, cornerstones optional.
- Frame each block and then add sashing strips, cornerstones optional.
- Blocks on-point in any of the ways above.
- Medallion-style.
- Blocks in an irregular setting; for example, offset alternate rows by half or any fraction of the block size.

Your quilt should be constructed so that the outer edges of the blocks, sashing strips and borders are on the straight-of-grain (lengthwise or cross-wise) of the fabric. This includes setting triangles at the sides of quilts with blocks set on-point.

Bias edges stretch and become distorted easily, causing inaccuracies and waviness. This effect can easily become more pronounced with each border that is added unless care is taken to make precise measurements. Occasionally bias edges are unavoidable; in such cases, handle them as little as possible and stitch them in at the earliest opportunity.

ADDING COMPLEXITY AND VARIETY

See pages 36-37 for layout ideas for just 16 blocks. Make more blocks with additional block types to create increasingly complex designs. Add sashing strips or set the blocks on-point to generate an even greater variety of patterns.

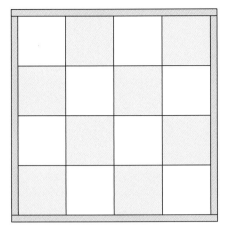

Blocks Set Square and Adjacent

Blocks Set Square with Sashing Strips

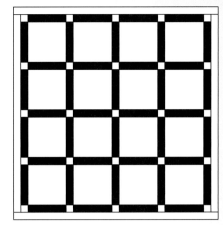

Blocks Set Square with Sashing and Corner-stones at Intersections

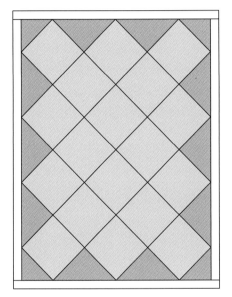

Blocks Set On-Point and Adjacent

Blocks Set On-Point with Sashing Strips

Blocks Set On-Point with Sashing and Corner-stone at Intersections

Assembling the Quilt

When joining the Bargello blocks, sometimes the seams of adjacent blocks match exactly; at other times they do not. When they match, take extra care to sew the seams accurately, pinning at each intersection. When the seams of adjacent blocks do not match, you won't have any matching intersections within the block to pin.

Sashing Strips

When you add sashing strips onto blocks, always press the seam allowances away from the blocks and toward the sashing strips. The same applies for frames and outer borders. If you add cornerstones to the sashing strips, press the seam allowances toward the sashing strips. Then, when you join all the pieces, the seam allowances will butt in opposing directions and there will be no bulky intersections.

Always stitch in an order that allows you to sew in straight lines without insetting any seams. Assemble your blocks in rows with their sashing strips, then join the rows together with the sashing strips that separate the rows. I find it helpful to number my patchwork pieces with small sticky labels to keep them in the correct order while sewing. Avoid ironing over the labels as the heat can make the glue extra sticky, which may leave a residue on the fabric.

Blocks Set On-Point

For blocks set on-point, these rows will be on the diagonal and have setting triangles on the outer edges. When sewing the setting triangles onto the blocks, align the right-angled corner of the triangle with the corner of the block and stitch toward the 45-degree triangle point. The 45-degree point will extend beyond the block and may be trimmed from the seam allowance after the diagonal rows are assembled. The corner triangles should be centered on the blocks so that there are excess triangles at each end. If the setting triangles and corners were originally cut larger than needed, the edges of the center field may be irregular. Trim them so that you have an accurate ¼" seam allowance all the way around. (See diagram on next page.)

Adjacent blocks and seams match

Adjacent blocks and seams do not match

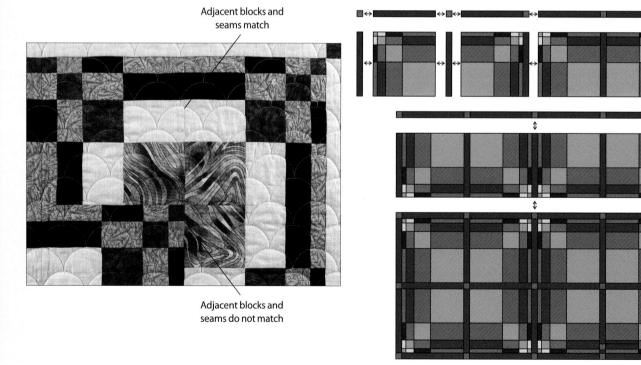

Sashing Strips

Assembling and Trimming On-Point Blocks with Setting Triangles

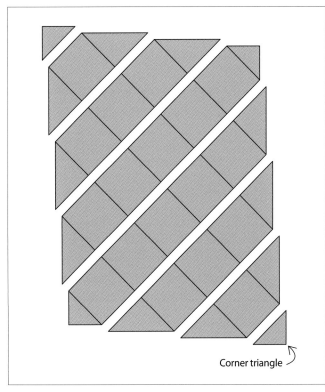

Adjacent Blocks   *Join in diagonal rows. Assemble rows.*

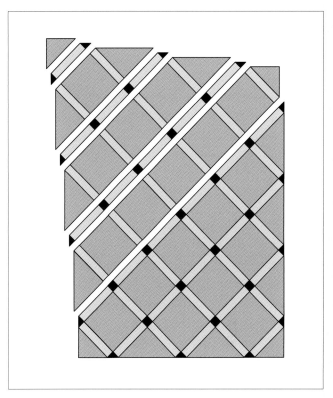

Blocks with Sashing Strips and Cornerstones   *Join in diagonal rows. Assemble rows.*

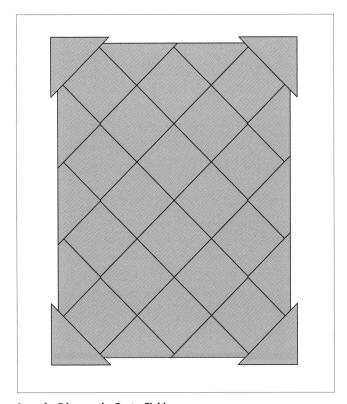

Irregular Edges on the Center Field

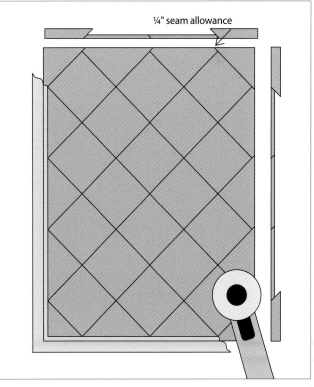

Trim to Leave ¼" Seam Allowance   *Borders will meet the corners of the blocks.*

Adding Borders

When adding borders that are not mitered, attach two opposite sides to the quilt top; then join the remaining borders with or without cornerstones. **Always measure the width and length across the center of the quilt top, not the edge** (which tends to distort). Use this to calculate the size of the strips to cut for the border.

For example, if the unfinished size of the quilt top (measured across the center) is 48" × 36" and you want to add a 2½" border, cut the side border strips 48" × 3". If your seam allowance is an accurate ¼", the top and bottom strips will be 41" × 3" (36" + 3" + 3" - 1" for four ¼" seam allowances). If your seam allowance may be inaccurate, measure the quilt after adding the side strips and use this measurement for the top and bottom strips. For multiple borders, add each border separately, measuring at each stage.

Avoiding Waves

The quilt top edge may be a little longer or shorter than the border. Ease or stretch the quilt top to fit the border by distributing the excess evenly along the entire seam length. See page 42 for instructions on pinning. Double-check your measurements if the discrepancy is large.

If a border is longer than the full width of the fabric (40-42"), you can cut it lengthwise from the fabric or piece it. To piece border strips, use a 45-degree angle seam and try to match up the fabric. This is less visible than a straight seam. For narrow strips in monochromatic tonal or small prints, a straight seam is fine. Taking the time to tackle this stage carefully and precisely is well worthwhile, even though you may be overeager to finish the project.

Mitering Corners on Borders

Mitered corners add a professional-looking touch to your quilt, especially on quilts that have multiple border strips. For multiple borders, first join the border strips together, so that when you attach them to the quilt, you can miter all of them at once.

---

1. Measure the quilt across the middle (not along the sides) in both directions. Cut the borders this length, plus 2 times their width, plus about 3" extra to allow plenty of fabric to accommodate the mitered corners.

   For example, if the finished quilt center = 41" × 51", and the finished border width = 3", then cut the borders: 2 @ 41 + (2 × 3") + 3" = 50" and 2 @ 51 + (2 × 3") + 3" = 60".

2. Center the border strips. Measure and mark with a pencil or pin the dimension of the quilt side minus ¼" at each end.

3. Pin 2 opposite borders before sewing. Position your mark at each end ¼" from the corners of the top. If the sides of your quilt are distorted, the border piece may not be exactly the same size. You must ease in any excess evenly and make it fit (see page 42).

4. Start sewing ½" to 1" away from the mark, first back-stitching to the mark but not beyond it.

   Stitch along the length of the side until you reach the mark at the other end, but do not stitch beyond it. Back-stitch 3 or 4 stitches. Attach the opposite side in the same way. Press the seam allowances towards the border strip.

5. Pin and sew the other 2 sides. When you reach the corners, be careful not to stitch onto the 2 border strips that are already attached. Press the seam allowances as above.

6. Use a pencil or chalk to mark the miters at each corner on the wrong side of each border section. Find the 45-degree angle on your ruler and line this up with the seam line, or use a mitering ruler. The edge of the ruler should be in the corner exactly where your stitching line ends. Make sure the border section is flat and straight before marking.

7. Carefully pin the corners matching the marked lines on the 2 pieces.

Extra care will be needed if you have multiple strips in your border, since these must match exactly when they are joined. Backstitch 3 or 4 stitches into the corner where the border joins the quilt, but not beyond it, and then stitch to the outer edge. Check that your seam is accurate before you cut away the excess fabric. The seam allowance may be pressed to one side or pressed open.

Mitered Corner on Bainbridge Delft   *Project quilt, page 92.*

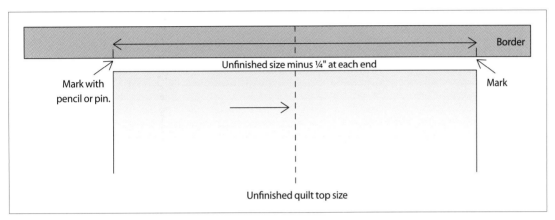

Mark Measurements on Border Strips

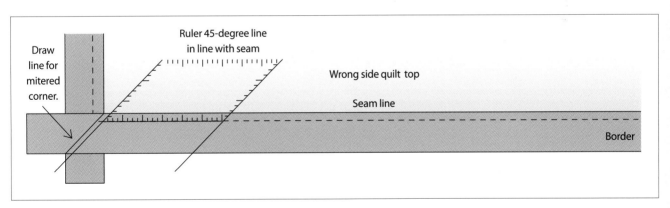

Mark Mitered Corners

Border Options

Like most stages of quilt making, there are many options for borders. This gallery illustrates various possibilities. Use these for ideas, and feel free to design your own to fit the character of your quilt.

Log Cabin-Style Borders   *Field of Flowers (project quilt, page 114).*

Border Strips with Cornerstones   *Gothic Medallion (project quilt, page 94).*

Mitered Corners   *Deck of Pansies (project quilt, page 74).*

Alternate Two Outer Border Fabrics, Extend the Bargello Pattern Into the Inner Border   *Mayan Mystery (project quilt, page 70).*

Alternate Two Outer Border Fabrics, Join at 45-Degree Angle *Autumn Harvest (project quilt, page 78).*

Cut Segments from Leftover Strip Sets to Make Pieced Borders *Savannah Sunrise (project quilt, page 104).*

Use Partial Bargello Blocks as Cornerstones *Pansy Picnic (Gallery quilt, page 63).*

Feature the Theme Fabric in Wide Border Panels *Edwardian Garden (project quilt, page 130).*

chapter 3

SMALL QUILTS AND PROJECTS

Beginning with a small project is a great introduction to the Bargello block technique. The projects in this chapter include a 16-block quilt to take you through the steps; a 20-block baby quilt; a table runner of 12 blocks with sashing; and a wall hanging of 16 blocks with sashing.

These quilts are quick and easy to piece. My students always begin by making 16 blocks, and they are amazed at the variety of patterns they are able to create by rotating and changing the orientation of the blocks. The addition of sashing strips and cornerstones further changes and expands the design possibilities. Notice the difference the sashing makes and how the fabric choices enhance the design.

Check out the Gallery at the end of the chapter to view and become inspired by some of the many possibilities using the Bargello block. I encourage you to play with your blocks, experimenting with color placement and patterns. Once you get started, you might decide to make more blocks and add on to your quilt.

Subsequent chapters provide guidance for quilts with more blocks.

Courtyard Fountains: *16-Block Quilt*

QUADRANGLE SETTING • QUILT SIZE: 35" × 35" • BLOCK SIZE: 7"

MATERIALS LIST

- ⅔ yard multistreaks for blocks and borders
- ⅔ yard blue for blocks, cornerstones and binding
- ½ yard lime green for blocks and borders
- ½ yard black for blocks

- ½ yard orange for blocks
- 39" × 39" batting
- 39" × 39" backing fabric

Initiate your creativity with the new Bargello block by beginning with this simple 16-block project. All the 7" blocks are the same in this 35" × 35" quilt. Once you've mastered the technique, you'll be stitching additional block designs and generating more innovative patterns and larger quilts.

In the Quadrangle setting of Courtyard Fountains, the large **A1** squares in the blocks come together at the center, framed by the **A2** and **B1** pieces. The center of the four **A1** squares is 6" × 6", so be careful when choosing the fabric for these squares. An option is to fussy-cut the **A1** squares (see page 39).

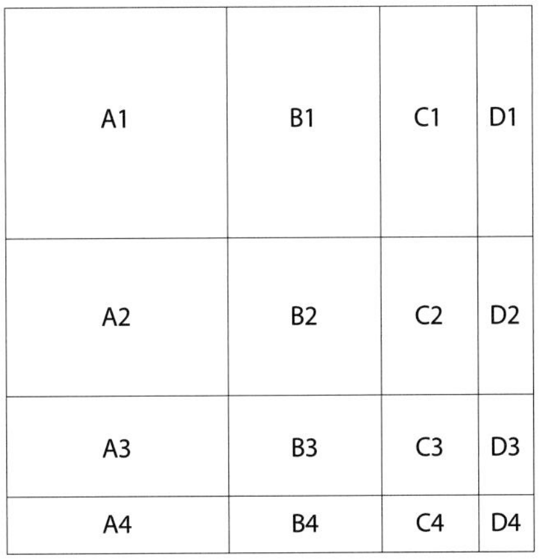

A1	B1	C1	D1
A2	B2	C2	D2
A3	B3	C3	D3
A4	B4	C4	D4

Bargello Block Diagram

Courtyard Fountains Block

Required: 16 blocks.

Constructing Courtyard Fountains

1. Piece the 16 blocks as instructed in Chapter Two. You should have 2 **A** strip sets and 1 each of the **B**, **C** and **D** sets before you make the counter-cuts. Counter-cut the **A** sets 3½", the **B** set 2½", the **C** set 1¾" and the **D** set 1¼": 16 segments of each. Join the segments to complete the blocks.

2. Lay out the blocks in the desired configuration; use the photograph as a guide or make your own pattern. Review the examples in the Gallery for further ideas. Assemble the center field of the quilt, joining the blocks in rows (see page 46). The center field should measure 28½" × 28½" across the middle. If the measurement differs, adjust the length of the border strips accordingly (see page 48).

3. Cut the 4 lime green inner border strips (28½" × 1¼") and the 4 blue cornerstones (1¼" × 1¼"). Cut the 4 multistreaked outer border strips (30" × 3") and the 4 blue cornerstones (3" × 3"). Add each border in turn, joining the 2 side strips first, then the tops and bottoms with the cornerstones attached (see page 48).

4. Baste, quilt and bind as directed in Chapter One. This quilt has an overall scalloped quilting pattern.

CUTTING FOR 16 BLOCKS

Note: Cut strips across the full width of the fabric, selvage to selvage (40").

Fabric	Block Part	No. of Strips	Size
Multistreaks	**A1**	2	3½" × 40"
Blue	**B2**	1	2½" × 40"
	C3	1	1¾" × 40"
	D4	1	1¼" × 40"
Lime Green	**A2**	2	2½" × 40"
	B1	1	3½" × 40"
Black	**A3**	2	1¾" × 40"
	C1	1	3½" × 40"
	B4	1	1¼" × 40"
	D2	1	2½" × 40"
Orange	**A4**	2	1¼" × 40"
	B3	1	1¾" × 40"
	C2	1	2½" × 40"
	D1	1	3½" × 40"
	C4	1	1¼" × 40"
	D3	1	1¾" × 40"

Star Light, Star Bright: 20-Block Baby Quilt

STEPS AND LADDERS SETTING • QUILT SIZE: 43" × 36" • BLOCK SIZE: 7"

MATERIALS LIST

- ½ yard sun, moon, stars for blocks
- ½ yard red for blocks
- ½ yard yellow for blocks and borders
- ½ yard blue for blocks
- ¼ yard lime green for blocks

- ⅔ yard stars on black for blocks and borders and ⅓ yard for binding
- 47" × 40" batting
- 47" × 40" backing fabric

This colorful star-spangled quilt of bright primary colors will add an attractive accent to the baby's room.

The orientation of the blocks creates the look of a series of steps and ladders. There are only six fabrics in the quilt. The blocks are set so that none of the pieces on adjacent blocks need to be exactly matched. This 20-block quilt is a fast and easy project.

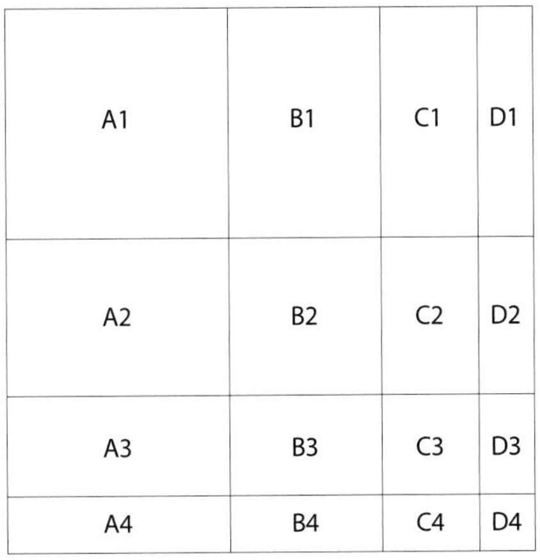

A1	B1	C1	D1
A2	B2	C2	D2
A3	B3	C3	D3
A4	B4	C4	D4

Bargello Block Diagram

Star Light, Star Bright Block
Required: 20 blocks.

Constructing Star Light, Star Bright

1. Piece the 20 blocks as instructed in Chapter Two. You should have 2 **A** strip sets, 2 **B** strip sets and 1 each of **C** and **D** before you make the counter-cuts. Counter-cut the **A** sets 3½", the **B** sets 2½", the **C** set 1¾" and the **D** set 1¼": 20 segments of each. Join the segments to complete the blocks.

2. Lay out the blocks in the desired configuration; use the photograph as a guide or make your own pattern. Assemble the center field of the quilt, joining the blocks in rows (see page 46). The center field should measure 35½" × 28½" across the middle. If the measurement differs, adjust the length of the border strips accordingly (see page 48).

3. Cut the yellow inner borders, 2 sides (35½" × 1¼") and the top and bottom (30" × 1¼"). Cut the stars on black outer borders, 2 sides (37" × 3½") and the top and bottom (36" × 3½"). Add each border in turn, joining the sides first, then the tops and bottoms (see page 48).

4. Baste, quilt and bind as directed in Chapter One. This quilt has an overall quilting pattern of stars joined with curly loops.

CUTTING FOR 20 BLOCKS

Note: Cut strips across the full width of the fabric, selvage to selvage (40").

Fabric	Block Part	No. of Strips	Size
Sun, Moon	A1	2	3½" × 40"
Stars	B2	2	2½" × 40"
Red	A2	2	2½" × 40"
	B1	2	3½" × 40"
Yellow	A3	2	1¾" × 40"
	C1	1	3½" × 40"
	D4	1	1¼" × 40"
Blue	A4	2	1¼" × 40"
	B3	2	1¾" × 40"
	C2	1	2½" × 40"
	D1	1	3½" × 40"
Lime Green	B4	2	1¼" × 40"
	C3	1	1¾" × 40"
	D2	1	2½" × 40"
Stars on	C4	1	1¼" × 40"
Black	D3	1	1¾" × 40"

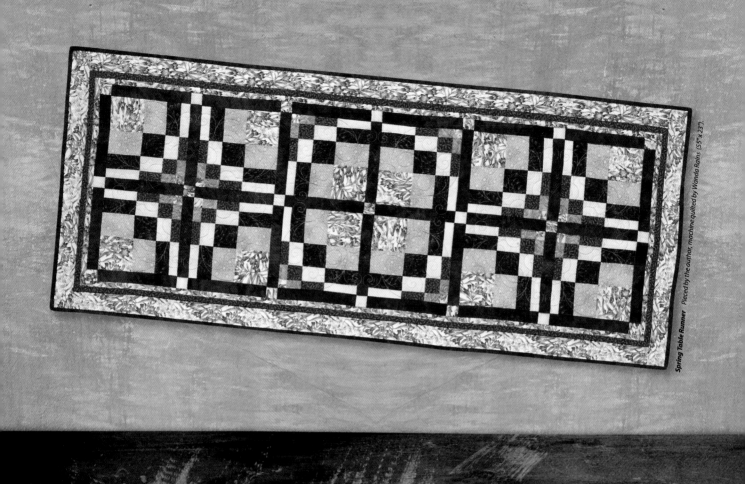

Spring Table Runner Pieced by the author, machine quilted by Wanda Rains. (55" x 23").

Spring Table Runner: 12 Bargello Blocks

WITH SASHING • QUILT SIZE: 55" × 23" • BLOCK SIZE: 7"

MATERIALS LIST

- 2¼ yards floral for blocks, cornerstones, borders and backing
- ¼ yard light purple for blocks
- ⅓ yard dark purple for blocks
- ⅓ yard yellow for blocks and cornerstones

- ½ yard green leaf for blocks and sashing
- ⅛ yard green swirl for blocks
- 1 yard magenta for sashing and binding
- 59" × 27" batting

Bring spring into your dining room with this floral table runner, or use it as a dresser topper. There are plenty of choices for matching the colors in your table settings to help feature this pretty piece.

The table runner has 12 Bargello blocks with sashing. The sashing adds a new dimension and breaks up the area where the four large **A1** squares come together. There are six fabrics

in the block. The addition of the rich magenta sashing helps to highlight the blocks and forms an integral part of the design.

58

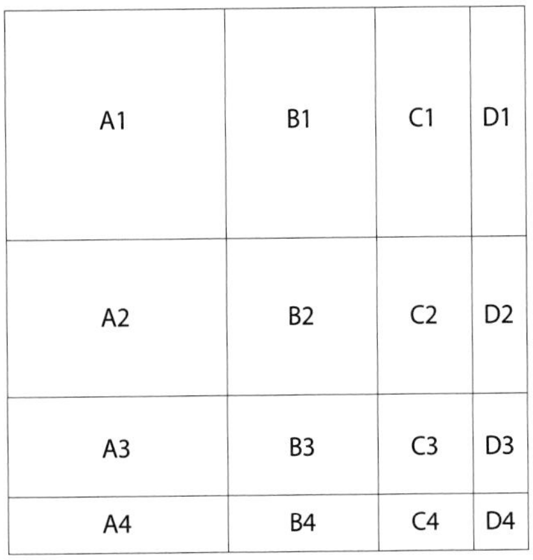

A1	B1	C1	D1
A2	B2	C2	D2
A3	B3	C3	D3
A4	B4	C4	D4

Bargello Block Diagram

Spring Table Runner Block
Required: 12 blocks.

Constructing Spring Table Runner

1. Piece the 12 blocks as instructed in Chapter Two. Counter-cut the **A** set 3½", the **B** set 2½", the **C** set 1¾" and the **D** set 1¼": 12 segments of each. The **A** strip set will only yield 11 **A** segments and you need 12. Use leftovers from the **B** strip set to make the 12th segment (see page 40). Join the segments to complete the blocks.

2. Cut the 32 magenta sashing strips (1½" × 7½") from 7 full-width strips; cut the 10 yellow and 11 floral 1½" × 1½" cornerstones. Lay out the blocks, sashing strips and cornerstones in the desired configuration; use the photograph as a guide or make your own pattern.

3. Assemble the center field of the quilt, joining the blocks, sashing strips and cornerstones in rows (see page 46). The center field should measure 49½" × 17½" across the middle. If the measurement differs, adjust the length of the border strips accordingly (see page 48).

4. Cut the inner and outer border strips lengthwise from 59" of the floral fabric, and trim them to the correct length. Inner border: cut 2 sides (49½" × 1"), and top and bottom (18½" × 1"). Outer border: cut 2 sides (51½" × 2¼"), and top and bottom (23" × 2¼"). Use the leftover 59" piece for the quilt back. Join strips for the green middle border sides unless you have enough fabric to cut them length-wise. Middle border: cut 2 sides (50½" × 1"), and top and bottom (19½" × 1"). Add each border in turn, joining the sides first, then the tops and bottoms (see page 48).

5. Baste, quilt and bind as directed in Chapter One. The table runner has a beautiful curlicue quilting pattern extending across each grouping of 4 blocks.

CUTTING FOR 12 BLOCKS

Note: Cut strips across the full width of the fabric, selvage to selvage (40").

Fabric	Block Part	No. of Strips	Size
Floral	A1	1	3½" × 40"
	D4	1	1¼" × 40"
Light Purple	A2	1	2½" × 40"
	B1	1	3½" × 40"
Dark Purple	A3	1	1¾" × 40"
	B2	1	2½" × 40"
	C1	1	3½" × 40"
Yellow	A4	1	1¼" × 40"
	B3	1	1¾" × 40"
	C2	1	2½" × 40"
	D1	1	3½" × 40"
Green Leaf	B4	1	1¼" × 40"
	C3	1	1¾" × 40"
	D2	1	2½" × 40"
Green Swirl	C4	1	1¼" × 40"
	D3	1	1¾" × 40"

Taste of Autumn Pieced by the author, machine quilted by Wanda Rains (39½" × 39½").

Taste of Autumn: 16-Block Quilt

WITH SASHING • QUILT SIZE: 39½" × 39½" • BLOCK SIZE: 7"

MATERIALS LIST

- ¾ yard multifeathers for blocks and borders
- ⅓ yard gold wings for blocks, cornerstones and borders
- 1 yard dark brown for blocks, sashing and borders
- ½ yard lime green for blocks and cornerstones
- ¼ yard light beige for blocks and sashing

- ¼ yard rust for blocks and cornerstones and ⅓ yard for binding
- ¼ yard light beige for blocks and sashing
- 44" × 44" batting
- 44" × 44" backing fabric

Imagine looking through a window on a blustery fall day to see swirls of colors and dark tree trunks. The sashing forms windowpane frames and provides a sense of depth and transparency. Liven up your wall or table with this seasonal quilt.

Like the last pattern, the sashing is an integral part of the design of this quilt made from 16 Bargello blocks. Notice how the choice of colors in the sashing and cornerstones produces a transparency effect and a continuation of the secondary pattern formed by the lime green.

60

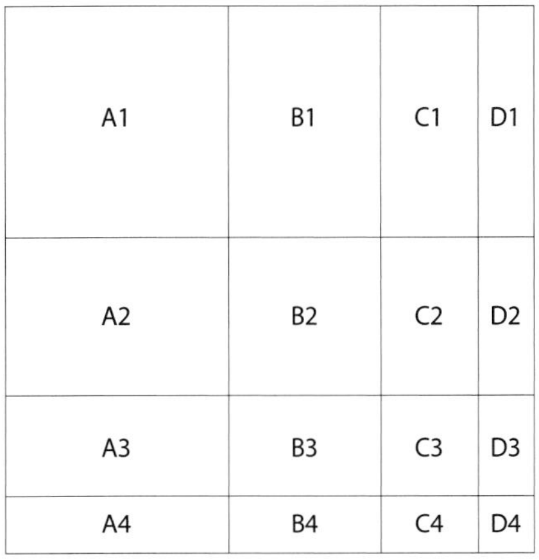

A1	B1	C1	D1
A2	B2	C2	D2
A3	B3	C3	D3
A4	B4	C4	D4

Bargello Block Diagram

Taste of Autumn Block

Required: 16 blocks.

Constructing Taste of Autumn

1. Piece the 16 blocks as instructed in Chapter Two. You should have 2 **A** strip sets and 1 each of **B**, **C** and **D** before you make the counter-cuts. Counter-cut the **A** sets 3½", the **B** set 2½", the **C** set 1¾" and the **D** set 1¼": 16 segments of each. Join the segments to complete the blocks.

2. Cut 32 dark brown sashing strips (1½" × 7½") from 7 full-width strips, and 8 light beige sashing strips (1½" × 7½") from 2 full-width strips. Cut 1½" × 1½" cornerstones: 13 rust, 8 lime green and 4 gold wings. Lay out the blocks, sashing strips and cornerstones in the desired configuration; use the photograph as a guide or make your own pattern.

3. Assemble the center field of the quilt, joining the blocks, sashing strips and cornerstones in rows (see page 46). The center field should be 33½" × 33½" across the middle. If the measurement differs, adjust the length of the border strips accordingly (see page 48).

4. Cut the border strips and cornerstones. For the inner feather border strips: cut four 33½" × 1½". For the inner gold wings cornerstones: cut four 1½" × 1½". For the outer dark brown border strips: cut four 35½" × 2½". For the outer feather cornerstones: cut four 2½" × 2½". Add each border in turn, joining the sides first, then the tops and bottoms with cornerstones on each end (see page 48).

5. For the quilt back, one width of fabric (42") may be sufficient. However, this will give you only a 1¼" buffer around the quilt top, so take extra care to accurately layer the quilt sandwich. Baste, quilt and bind as directed in Chapter One. The quilting pattern is feathery swirls evoking tumbling windblown leaves.

CUTTING FOR 16 BLOCKS			
Note: Cut strips across the full width of the fabric, selvage to selvage (40").			
Fabric	**Block Part**	**No. of Strips**	**Size**
Feathers	A1	2	3½" × 40"
	B2	1	2½" × 40"
	C3	1	1¾" × 40"
	D4	1	1¼" × 40"
Gold Wings	A2	2	2½" × 40"
	B1	1	3½" × 40"
Dark Brown	A3	2	1¾" × 40"
	C1	1	3½" × 40"
Lime Green	A4	2	1¼" × 40"
	B3	1	1¾" × 40"
	C2	1	2½" × 40"
	D1	1	3½" × 40"
Rust	B4	1	1¼" × 40"
	D2	1	2½" × 40"
Light Beige	C4	1	1¼" × 40"
	D3	1	1¾" × 40"

Bargello Circles *Quadrangle setting. Made by Linda Johnston (36" × 36").*

Compare this quilt with Courtyard Fountains (page 54). The Quadrangle setting is the same, but because of the fabric choices and value placements in the blocks, it looks very different. This beautifully illustrates how placement of value and color in the block can change the outcome.

In Bargello Circles, the dark purple **A4-B3-C2-D1** arcs are in high contrast to other medium and light prints. The variety of print scales and textures adds interest to the light areas within the purple circles.

Buon Natale *Quadrangle setting. Made by Barbara Micheal (39" × 39").*

Like Courtyard Fountains (page 54), Buon Natale also uses the Quadrangle setting. Again, fabric choices and value placements in the blocks create a different effect. The red **A2** and **B1** pieces stand out, framing the groupings of **A1** squares. Notice the addition of the pieced border from leftover strip sets to complete this attractive Christmas quilt.

Pansy Picnic *Quadrangle setting with side blocks reversed. Pieced by the author, machine quilted by Wanda Rains (36" × 36").*

Pansy Picnic is almost the same Quadrangle setting, but the outer side blocks are turned so that the **A1** squares are toward the center instead of the corners. Partial blocks form the cornerstones of the borders.

Rambling Roses *Made by the author (36½" × 36½").*

The corner blocks in Rambling Roses are set just like those in Pansy Picnic (above), but the four inner blocks are turned so that the small **D4** squares come together in the center. In this setting, the rose fabric in the **A1**, **B2**, **C3** and **D4** squares forms a diagonal secondary pattern across the quilt.

63

Chasing Butterflies *Tessellated Butterfly setting. Pieced by the author, machine quilted by Wanda Rains (36" × 36").*

The tessellated butterflies are outlined by the turquoise **A4-B3-C2-D1** arcs that join at the block boundaries to create this secondary pattern. Notice how the black **C4** and **D3** pieces stand out against the adjacent yellow contrasting fabric. The inner pieced border is made from segments cut from leftover strip sets.

Bubble Gum Confection *Straight Furrows setting. Made by Carol Graves (36" × 36").*

In the Straight Furrows setting, the blocks are arranged so that diagonal lines of color extend across the quilt top, like those in a traditional Log Cabin Straight Furrows quilt. Here the pink and turquoise in Bubble Gum Confection form continuous zigzags sandwiching the other fabrics and their diagonal patterns.

Bedtime Butterflies *Tessellated Butterfly setting with fleece backing. Pieced by the author, machine quilted by Wanda Rains (43" × 36"). Fabric from the "Butterflies and Flowers" line by David Textiles Inc., designed by the author and Beth Bruske.*

Like Star Light, Star Bright (page 56), this charming baby quilt has 20 Bargello blocks all of one type, and the border sizes are the same. The blocks are set so that none of the pieces on adjacent blocks need to be matched, which makes the quilt assembly fast and easy. It is backed with soft fleece and does not contain batting. If you use a fleece backing, be careful not to stretch it during quilting.

Destination *Quadrangle setting with sashing. Pieced by Christine Johnson, machine quilted by Wanda Rains (45" × 45").*

Compare this quilt with Pansy Picnic (page 63). The setting is similar apart from the four corner blocks, which are turned so that the **A1** squares are on the outer edge. Of course, the addition of sashing changes the design, which is augmented by the wonderful variety of print scales and rich textures. Although the color palette is similar to the project quilt Taste of Autumn (page 60), the two look very different.

Mom's Heavenly Garden *Tessellated Butterfly setting with sashing made from leftover strip sets. Made by Valerie Martinson (41" × 41").*

In this quilt, the tessellated butterflies are slightly visible, outlined by the red and pink **A4**-**B3**-**C2**-**D1** arcs. However, the pieced sashing interrupts the continuous flow, and the blocks merge so that it is hard to tell where one ends and the next begins. The sashing strips are made from segments cut from the leftover **C** and **D** sets. These create new patterns in the quilt, the most noticeable being where the purple **D2** pieces are adjacent to the **D2** pieces in the blocks. This creates little purple accents on the quilt.

A Few Flowers for the Garden *Tessellated Butterfly setting with sashing. Made by Klina Dupuy (48½" × 48½").*

*It's hard to believe that this quilt is the Tessellated Butterfly setting. The **A4-B3-C2-D1** arcs are made up of different fabrics so the butterflies are no longer outlined; they disappear. The 16 blocks are grouped into four mega-blocks (a large block made up of four regular blocks). The hot pink **B2**, **C3** and **D4** squares and **A1** flowers pop out and form an interesting diagonal secondary pattern. These two fabrics are featured in the creatively placed sashing strips, which play a huge role in the overall design of the quilt. With the split sashing and alternating floral and pink cornerstones, a 4-patch appears in the middle, linking the diagonal patterns in the mega-blocks.*

chapter 4

36-BLOCK QUILTS

All the quilts in this chapter are made from 36 blocks squarely set. As we increase the number of blocks and block types, the patterns become more sophisticated. This provides an excellent opportunity to combine a greater variety of fabrics, introducing more colors, different value placements and print sizes.

If you began by making 16 blocks and would like to make more for a larger quilt, consider making 20 with new fabric choices: two sets of eight and a set of four, or some other combination to make the total of 36 blocks. The projects and Gallery quilts show a variety of options. Some use 36 blocks that are all the same, while others have as many as four different block types.

There are four projects, each featuring a different setting. These are named after traditional quilt patterns that I hope you will recognize: Trip Around the World, Card Trick and Straight Furrows, with the fourth project adding sashing strips in a Trip Around the World setting.

In Trip Around the World, the blocks are oriented to create an on-point concentric pattern in the same format as the traditional pattern that utilizes small squares. In the Card Trick setting, you will see the same overlapping look of fanned cards found in the traditional block of that name. Straight Furrows is a traditional setting for Log Cabin blocks; those rows or furrows are re-created with the Bargello blocks.

Mayan Mystery: 36-Block Quilt

TRIP AROUND THE WORLD SETTING • **QUILT SIZE: 53" × 53"** • **BLOCK SIZE: 7"**

MATERIALS LIST

- 1 yard orange batik for blocks, borders and binding
- 1½ yards dark batik for blocks, borders and binding
- 1¼ yards blue/purple hydrangea for blocks and borders
- ½ yard dark blue for blocks and borders

- ¾ yard yellow rain for blocks and borders
- ⅓ yard beige for blocks and borders
- 58" × 58" batting
- 58" × 58" backing fabric

Traditional Trip Around the World quilts are made from many same-sized small squares with colors arranged in an on-point format, creating concentric waves of color radiating outwards. This Bargello block setting maintains the integrity of the design, but includes the squares of differing sizes and rectangles that constitute the block. You can easily create eye-catching quilts using this format.

Mayan Mystery has two block types: 18 with orange batik **A1** squares, and 18 with dark batik **A1** squares. I cut the **A1** squares for the blocks separately, adding them after I positioned all the other block parts on my work wall. This enabled me to manipulate the positioning of the batik prints, notably the dark ferny squares at the center of the quilt.

Apart from the **A1** squares, all 36 blocks are the same. Pieces **D3** and **D4** are made from the same fabric, so they may be combined into one patch. The inner border is pieced so that the pattern extends to complete the Trip Around the World pattern in the dark blue fabric. This also makes the corner sections look as though they float on the hydrangea print background.

A1	B1	C1	D1
A2	B2	C2	D2
A3	B3	C3	D3
A4	B4	C4	D4

Bargello Block Diagram

Constructing Mayan Mystery
(See the cutting charts on pages 72-73.)

1. Piece the 36 blocks as instructed in Chapter Two. Cut the **A1** squares separately and complete sections of the blocks as instructed on page 39. You should have 4 **A** strip sets, 3 **B** strip sets and 2 each of the others. Counter-cut the **A** sets 3½", the **B** sets 2½", the **C** sets 1¾" and the **D** sets 1¼": 36 segments of each. Your **A** segments will consist of **A2**, **A3** and **A4**, with separate **A1** squares; and the completed **B**, **C** and **D** segments should be joined into 1 piece.

2. Lay out the block segments and **A1** squares in the desired configuration; use the photograph as a guide or make your own pattern. You may experiment by cutting different **A1** squares to create a new look. Join the **A1** squares onto the **A** segments in the correct orientation, then complete the blocks. Assemble the center field of the quilt, joining the blocks in rows (see page 46). The completed center field should measure 42½" × 42½".

3. Cut the pieces for the inner border; see page 73. (Feel free to simplify the borders if you prefer.)

A 14" section in the middle of each border contains several pieces to extend the Trip Around the World pattern out toward the edge of the quilt.

Use the photo on page 73 as a guide to help you with the piecing order. Make 4 border strips.

Join the 1¼"-wide pieces end to end in the following sequence: yellow rain, dark blue, beige, dark blue, yellow rain. Make 4.

Join the 1¾" pieces end to end in the following sequence: blue/purple hydrangea, yellow rain, dark blue, yellow rain, blue/purple hydrangea. Make 4.

Sew each 1¼"-wide section to a 1¾"-wide section for a total width of 2½".

Cut the four 2½" × 40" blue/purple hydrangea strips in half and join each piece onto the ends of the pieced sections from above. Center the strips so that the pieced sections are in the correct positions on the sides of the quilt. Stitch and miter the corners (see page 48).

4. Cut the outer border strips: 4 dark batik (40" × 3¾") and 4 orange batik (40" × 3¾"). Join the short ends of the orange and dark batik strips. Center the seams on the sides of the quilt and miter the corners (see page 48).

5. Baste, quilt and bind as directed in Chapter One. The quilt has a diagonal grid of serpentine quilting stitches. See page 22 for a detailed photo. This striking pieced pattern with busy batik prints lends itself well to a simple overall pattern.

Orange Batik Block
Required: 18 blocks.

Dark Batik Block
Required: 18 blocks.

CUTTING FOR 18 ORANGE BATIK AND 18 DARK BATIK BLOCKS

Note: Cut strips across the full width of the fabric, selvage to selvage (40").

Cut **A1** 3½" squares separately (18 orange batik, 18 dark batik).

D3 and **D4** are combined into one strip.

Fabric	Block Part	No. of Strips	Size
Blue/Purple	**A2**	4	2½" × 40"
Hydrangea	**B1**	3	3½" × 40"
Dark Batik	**A3**	4	1¾" × 40"
	B2	3	2½" × 40"
	C1	2	3½" × 40"
Yellow Rain	**A4**	4	1¼" × 40"
	B3	3	1¾" × 40"
	C2	2	2½" × 40"
	D1	2	3½" × 40"
Dark Blue	**B4**	3	1¼" × 40"
	C3	2	1¾" × 40"
	D2	2	2½" × 40"
Beige	**C4**	2	1¼" × 40"
	D3/ D4	2	2½" × 40"

CUTTING FOR INNER PIECED BORDER

Fabric	No. of Pieces	Size
Blue/Purple	8	4½" × 1¾"
Hydrangea	4	2½" × 40"
Dark Blue	8	2½" × 1¼"
	4	2½" × 1¾"
	5	
Beige	4	2½" × 1¼"
Yellow Rain	8	4½" × 1¼"
	8	2½" × 1¾"

Detail of Pieced Border

Deck of Pansies: 36-Block Quilt

CARD TRICK SETTING • QUILT SIZE: 53" × 53" • BLOCK SIZE: 7"

MATERIALS LIST

- ½ yard pansies for blocks and borders
- 1 yard light gray for blocks
- 2 ¼ yards black dragonflies for blocks and borders
- 1½ yards red for blocks, borders and binding
- ¾ yard blue for blocks

- ⅔ yard yellow for blocks
- ¼ yard gray leaves for blocks
- 57" × 57" batting
- 57" × 57" backing fabric

This Card Trick setting is a stunning design. The use of primary colors with the black and light gray makes the pattern pop out, and the beautiful double-plume quilting stitches over the surface add to the richness. Enjoy manipulat-

ing your Bargello blocks to create this striking piece.

Deck of Pansies looks rather complicated, but the pattern may be easily broken down into the four component block types. The 12 pansy blocks form

the Card Trick pattern in the center; there are eight each of the other three block types.

Notice how the **A4-B3-C2-D1** yellow arc is the same in both the red and blue corner blocks, so that the arcs join and create large circles unifying and adding to the pattern.

With four block types, you need to stay well organized. I recommend cutting and piecing each block type in turn, to reduce confusing the strips.

A1	B1	C1	D1
A2	B2	C2	D2
A3	B3	C3	D3
A4	B4	C4	D4

Bargello Block Diagram

Constructing Deck of Pansies

(See the cutting charts on pages 76-77.)

1. Cut the long black dragonflies borders (see the pansy block cutting chart on page 76) before cutting the strips for the blocks. Piece the 36 blocks: 12 pansy blocks, 8 gray side blocks, 8 blue corner blocks and 8 red corner blocks, as instructed in Chapter Two. For all the block types, you should have one strip set of **A**, **B**, **C** and **D**. Counter-cut the **A** set 3½", the **B** set 2½", the **C** set 1¾" and the **D** set 1¼": 12 segments for the pansy blocks and 8 each for the other 3 block types.

2. For the pansy blocks, cut the **A1** squares separately and complete the sections of the blocks as instructed on page 39. Your **A** segments will consist of **A2**, **A3** and **A4**, with separate **A1** squares; and the completed **B**, **C** and **D** segments should be joined into 1 piece. The **A** strip set yields only 11 segments; you need 12. Use leftovers from the **B** strip set to make the 12th segment (see page 40).

3. Lay out the block segments, **A1** pansy squares and the other completed blocks in the desired configuration; use the photograph as a guide or make your own pattern. Join the **A1** squares onto the **A** segments in the correct orientation, then complete the pansy blocks. Assemble the center field of the quilt, joining the blocks in rows (see page 46). The completed center field should measure 42½" × 42½".

4. There are 4 borders with mitered corners. You should already have the second and outer black dragonflies border strips cut (see the pansy block cutting chart on page 76 for instructions). Trim the second border strips to 50" × 1¾". Cut and join strips for the inner red border to make four 50" × 1". Cut and join strips for the third pansy border to make four 50" × 1¼". Strip piece the inner, second and third border strips. Center these on the outer 55" black dragonflies strips and join. Attach them to the quilt top, mitering the corners (see page 48). As an alternative, add each border in turn, joining the sides first, then the tops and bottoms (see page 48).

5. Baste, quilt and bind as directed in Chapter One. Deck of Pansies has a spectacular overall double-plume quilting pattern stitched with variegated black, gray and white thread. This greatly enhances the quilt and is particularly visible on the black borders (see photo on opposite page and on page 50).

REDUCING WASTAGE

To economize on fabric for the block types with eight blocks, use just half a strip (20") for the **C** and **D** sets. Half a **D** set is also sufficient for the 12 pansy blocks. If you cut and piece each block type in turn, you can use some of the leftover strip halves for the next block type, thereby reducing your cutting, sewing and fabric wastage.

Pansy Block
Required: 12 blocks.

Gray Side Block
Required: 8 blocks.

CUTTING FOR 12 PANSY BLOCKS

Note: Cut strips across the full width of the fabric, selvage to selvage (40"), except for black dragonflies.

Black dragonflies: First cut 4 outer border strips (3½") and 4 second border strips (1¾") lengthwise from 55" fabric; then cut strips for blocks from the remaining pieces.

Fussy-cut 12 **A1** pansy squares 3½" × 3½".

Fabric	Block Part	No. of Strips	Size
Light Gray	A2	1	2½" × 40"
	B1	1	3½" × 40"
Black Dragonflies	A3	1	1¾" × 40"
	B2	1	2½" × 40"
	C1	1	3½" × 40"
	B4	1	1¼" × 40"
	C3	1	1¾" × 40"
	D2	1	2½" × 40"
	D4	1	1¼" × 40"
Red	A4	1	1¼" × 40"
	B3	1	1¾" × 40"
	C2	1	2½" × 40"
	D1	1	3½" × 40"
Blue	C4	1	1¼" × 40"
	D3	1	1¾" × 40"

CUTTING FOR 8 GRAY SIDE BLOCKS

Note: Cut strips across the full width of the fabric, selvage to selvage (40"), except for black dragonflies.

Fabric	Block Part	No. of Strips	Size
Blue	A1	1	3½" × 40"
Gray Leaves	A2	1	2½" × 40"
	B1	1	3½" × 40"
Red	A3	1	1¾" × 40"
	B2	1	2½" × 40"
	C1	1	3½" × 40"
Light Gray	A4	1	1¼" × 40"
	B3	1	1¾" × 40"
	C2	1	2½" × 40"
	D1	1	3½" × 40"
	C4	1	1¼" × 40"
	D3	1	1¾" × 40"
Black Dragonflies	B4	1	1¼" × 40"
	C3	1	1¾" × 40"
	D2	1	2½" × 40"
	D4	1	1¼" × 40"

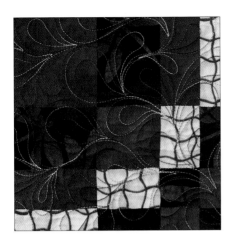

Blue Corner Block
Required: 8 blocks.

Red Corner Block
Required: 8 blocks.

CUTTING FOR 8 BLUE CORNER BLOCKS

Note: Cut strips across the full width of the fabric, selvage to selvage (40"), except for black dragonflies.

Fabric	Block Part	No. of Strips	Size
Blue	A1	1	3½" × 40"
	A3	1	1¾" × 40"
	B2	1	2½" × 40"
	C1	1	3½" × 40"
	C4	1	1¼" × 40"
	D3	1	1¾" × 40"
Black	A2	1	2½" × 40"
Dragonflies	B1	1	3½" × 40"
	B4	1	1¼" × 40"
	C3	1	1¾" × 40"
	D2	1	2½" × 40"
	D4	1	1¼" × 40"
Yellow	A4	1	1¼" × 40"
	B3	1	1¾" × 40"
	C2	1	2½" × 40"
	D1	1	3½" × 40"

CUTTING FOR 8 RED CORNER BLOCKS

Note: Cut strips across the full width of the fabric, selvage to selvage (40"), except for black dragonflies.

Fabric	Block Part	No. of Strips	Size
Red	A1	1	3½" × 40"
	B2	1	2½" × 40"
	C3	1	1¾" × 40"
	D4	1	1¼" × 40"
Light Gray	A2	1	2½" × 40"
	B1	1	3½" × 40"
Black	A3	1	1¾" × 40"
Dragonflies	C1	1	3½" × 40"
	B4	1	1¼" × 40"
	D2	1	2½" × 40"
Yellow	A4	1	1¼" × 40"
	B3	1	1¾" × 40"
	C2	1	2½" × 40"
	D1	1	3½" × 40"
Blue	C4	1	1¼" × 40"
	D3	1	1¾" × 40"

Autumn Harvest   Pieced by the author, machine quilted by Wanda Rains (54" × 54").

Autumn Harvest: 36-Block Quilt

STRAIGHT FURROWS SETTING • QUILT SIZE: 54" × 54" • BLOCK SIZE: 7"

MATERIALS LIST

- ⅓ yard blue/multi floral for blocks
- ¾ yard brown leaves for blocks and borders
- 1 yard dark brown woven for blocks, borders and binding
- ¼ yard beige scroll for blocks
- ¼ yard maroon small floral for blocks
- ⅛ yard yellow bubbles for blocks
- ¾ yard rust floral for blocks and borders
- ¾ yard gold leaves for blocks and borders
- ½ yard blue small floral for blocks
- ¼ yard beige flames for blocks

- ¼ yard maroon with black zigzag for blocks
- ⅛ yard yellow streaks for blocks
- ⅛ yard dark blue for **A1** squares in blocks
- ¼ yard brilliant blue for **A1** squares in blocks and borders
- ¼ yard beige large floral for **A1** squares in blocks
- 58" × 58" batting
- 58" × 58" backing fabric

The Straight Furrows setting is named after the similar traditional Log Cabin setting. It highlights the strong diagonal flow that looks like plowed furrows. These autumnal colors glow with the brilliant blue of the clear skies that we often enjoy in late September or early October.

Autumn Harvest has two block types: 17 brown and 19 gold. I cut the **A1** squares for all the blocks separately, adding them after I positioned all the other block parts on my work wall. The blues and beige large floral print **A1**s are arranged in diagonal lines consistent with the Straight Furrows theme. Feel free to simplify the pieced border.

A1	B1	C1	D1
A2	B2	C2	D2
A3	B3	C3	D3
A4	B4	C4	D4

Bargello Block Diagram

Constructing Autumn Harvest
(See the cutting charts on page 80.)

1. Piece the 2 types of blocks as instructed in Chapter Two: 17 brown and 19 gold. Counter-cut the **A** sets 3½", the **B** set 2½", the **C** set 1¾" and the **D** set 1¼": 17 segments of each for the brown blocks and 19 for the gold. I suggest cutting the **A1** squares separately and completing sections of the blocks as instructed on page 39. Your **A** segments will consist of **A2**, **A3** and **A4**, with separate **A1** squares; and the completed **B**, **C** and **D** segments should be joined into 1 piece. For the brown block type, you should have 2 **A** strip sets and 1 each of the others. The **B** strip set will yield only 16 segments; you need 17. Make the final segment from leftover scraps from the other strip sets (see page 40). For the gold block type, there are 2 strip sets for **A** and **B**, and 1 each for **C** and **D**.

2. Lay out the block segments and **A1** squares in the desired configuration; use the photograph as a guide or make your own pattern. You can experiment by cutting different **A1** squares to create a new look. Join the **A1** squares onto the **A** segments, then complete the blocks.

3. Assemble the center field of the quilt, joining the blocks in rows (see page 46). The completed center field should measure 42½" × 42½" across the center. If the measurement is different, adjust the length of the border strips accordingly (see page 48).

4. Add the inner pieced border, which consists of rust floral strips sandwiching leftovers, and blue cornerstones. Counter-cut the leftover strip sets into 1¼" segments. Join the segments to make four 44" strips. Cut nine 1½" full-width rust floral strips and piece them into 8 strips of 44" × 1½". Sew the rust floral strips on either side of the pieced scrappy strips. Trim to 42½" and stitch 2 of these border strips onto the sides. Cut four 3¼" × 3¼" blue cornerstones and join to each end of the other 2 border strips. Sew these onto the top and bottom. The quilt top should now measure 48" × 48" across the center.

5. Cut five 1" full-width dark brown strips and piece the middle borders, 2 sides (48" × 1") and the top and bottom (49" × 1"). Join onto the quilt top; first the sides, then the top and bottom.

6. For the outer border, cut four 40" × 2¾" strips each of the gold and brown fabrics. Join the gold and brown strips with a 45-degree seam aligned in the same direction as the diagonal orientation of the straight furrows. Center these seams and miter the corners (see page 48).

7. Baste, quilt and bind as directed in Chapter One. Autumn Harvest has a flowing diagonal quilting pattern with the occasional mini-whirlpool.

Brown Block
Required: 17 blocks.

Gold Block
Required: 19 blocks.

CUTTING FOR 17 BROWN BLOCKS

Note: Cut strips across the full width of the fabric, selvage to selvage (40").

Cut 3½" **A1** squares separately (4 dark blue, 5 brilliant blue, 8 beige large floral).

Fabric	Block Part	No. of Strips	Size
Blue/ Multifloral	**A2**	2	2½" × 40"
	B1	1	3½" × 40"
Brown Leaves	**A3**	2	1¾" × 40"
	B2	1	2½" × 40"
	C1	1	3½" × 40"
Dark Brown Woven	**A4**	2	1¼" × 40"
	B3	1	1¾" × 40"
	C2	1	2½" × 40"
	D1	1	3½" × 40"
Beige Scroll	**B4**	1	1¼" × 40"
	C3	1	1¾" × 40"
	D2	1	2½" × 40"
Maroon Small Floral	**C4**	1	1¼" × 40"
	D3	1	1¾" × 40"
Yellow Bubbles	**D4**	1	1¼" × 40"

CUTTING FOR 19 GOLD BLOCKS

Note: Cut strips across the full width of the fabric, selvage to selvage (40").

Cut 3½" **A1** squares separately (4 dark blue, 6 brilliant blue, 9 beige large floral).

Fabric	Block Part	No. of Strips	Size
Rust/Floral	**A2**	2	2½" × 40"
	B1	2	3½" × 40"
Gold Leaves	**A3**	2	1¾" × 40"
	B2	2	2½" × 40"
	C1	1	3½" × 40"
Blue Small Floral	**A4**	2	1¼" × 40"
	B3	2	1¾" × 40"
	C2	1	2½" × 40"
	D1	1	3½" × 40"
Beige Flames	**B4**	2	1¼" × 40"
	C3	1	1¾" × 40"
	D2	1	2½" × 40"
Maroon with Black Zigzag	**C4**	1	1¼" × 40"
	D3	1	1¾" × 40"
Yellow Streaks	**D4**	1	1¼" × 40"

Detail of Border

Reflections Pieced by Christine Johnson, machine quilted by Wanda Rains (53" × 53").

Reflections: 36-Block Quilt

WITH SASHING • QUILT SIZE: 53" × 53" • BLOCK SIZE: 7"

MATERIALS LIST

- 2 yards gray on black for blocks, sashing and borders
- ¾ yard brown tonal for blocks
- ¾ yard multicolored boxes for blocks
- 1⅓ yards orange for blocks and binding
- ½ yard lime green for blocks
- ¼ yard dark brown for blocks
- ¼ yard yellow for blocks and cornerstones
- 57" × 57" batting
- 57" × 57" backing fabric

This rich quilt with a lush-looking texture glows. It will add an electrifying accent on a wall as a hanging or over a couch as a lap quilt. The dark sashing strips intensify the colors, and the yellow cornerstones look like points of light. All 36 blocks are the same, so it is quick and simple to piece.

The fabric selections for the blocks include a wonderful range of values and textures, from very dark to neon, from multicolored boxes to subtle tonal prints. It almost looks like ultrasuede or velvet.

From this basic pattern of one block type with sashing, you could arrange the blocks in a variety of ways. Feel free to play around with the layout.

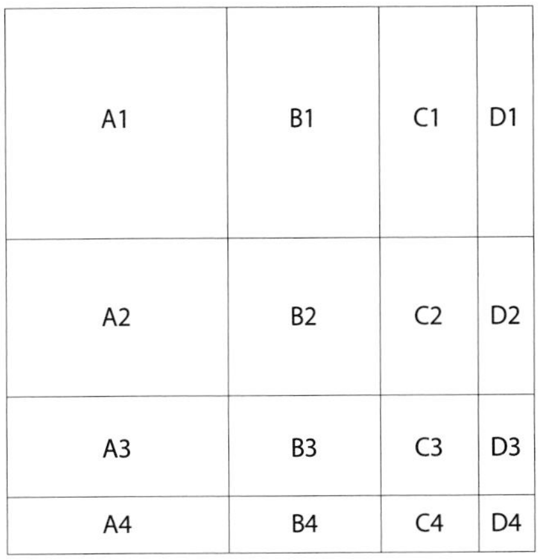

A1	B1	C1	D1
A2	B2	C2	D2
A3	B3	C3	D3
A4	B4	C4	D4

*Bargello Block
Diagram*

Reflections Block
Required: 36 blocks.

Constructing Reflections

1. Piece the 36 blocks as instructed in Chapter Two. All the blocks are the same. You should have 4 **A** strip sets, 3 **B** strip sets and 2 each of the others. Counter-cut the **A** sets 3½", the **B** sets 2½", the **C** sets 1¾" and the **D** sets 1¼": 36 segments of each. Join the segments to complete the blocks.

2. Cut the 4 gray on black border strips lengthwise from the fabric (54" × 3¼"). Use the leftover piece to cut 1¼" strips for the sashing. You will need 84 sashing strips (7½" × 1¼"). Cut 49 yellow cornerstones (1¼" × 1¼").

3. Lay out the blocks, sashing strips and cornerstones in the desired configuration; use the photograph as a guide or make your own pattern. Assemble the center field of the quilt, joining the components in rows (see page 46). The completed center field should measure 47¾" × 47¾" across the middle. If the measurement is different, adjust the length of the border strips accordingly (see page 48).

4. Trim the gray on black border strips: 2 for the sides (47¾" × 3¼") and 2 for the top and bottom (53¼" × 3¼"). Attach the side strips to the quilt top, then add the top and bottom strips. Alternatively, do not trim the border strips; instead, add them to the quilt top and miter the corners (see page 48).

5. Baste, quilt and bind as directed in Chapter One. Reflections has an on-point quilting pattern of straight lines and twisted ribbons.

CUTTING FOR 36 BLOCKS

Note: Cut strips across the full width of the fabric, selvage to selvage (40").

Fabric	Block Part	No. of Strips	Size
Gray on Black	**A1**	4	3½" × 40"
Brown Tonal	**A2**	4	2½" × 40"
	B1	3	3½" × 40"
Multicolored Boxes	**A3**	4	1¾" × 40"
	B2	3	2½" × 40"
	C1	2	3½" × 40"
Orange	**A4**	4	1¼" × 40"
	B3	3	1¾" × 40"
	C2	2	2½" × 40"
	D1	2	3½" × 40"
Lime Green	**B4**	3	1¼" × 40"
	C3	2	1¾" × 40"
	D2	2	2½" × 40"
Dark Brown	**C4**	2	1¼" × 40"
	D3	2	1¾" × 40"
Yellow	**D4**	2	1¼" × 40"

GALLERY

Garden Picnic   *Made by Jacque Noard*
(56" × 56").

*The purple really pops against the lime green, and the **A2** and **B1** pieces form wonderful loopy ribbons in this Trip Around the World format. All 36 blocks are the same. The fused appliquéd flowers in the corners add a nice touch to this vibrant piece.*

Fishgello   *Pieced by Carol Wood, machine quilted by Jacque Noard (50½" × 50½").*

*In Fishgello, the pattern is more subtle and muted because the fabrics are similar in value. The small pieces in the corners of the blocks (**B4**, **C3**, **D2**, **C4**, **D3** and **D4**) are much darker and provide the contrast, standing out sandwiched between the pale blue pieces. There are two block types: the four center blocks with fussy-cut fish **A1** squares form a focal medallion; the other 32 blocks provide a tranquil setting. The piecing extends out into the border to resolve the Trip Around the World pattern, and the binding is made from a variety of the fabrics.*

84

Dancing Cards *Pieced by the author, machine quilted by Wanda Rains (54½" × 54½").*

Dancing Cards is almost the same layout as Deck of Pansies (page 74). The only difference is the corners where the inner blocks are turned, so that three-quarter circles are formed instead of complete circles. There are four block types: 12 center blocks, 12 corner blocks, four inner corners and eight outer sides. Notice how the placement of the purple in the outer side and corner blocks blends with the border so that the design floats. The pieced pattern is extended into the border in the middle of each side to complete the fabric sequence.

Irregular Furrows   *Pieced by the author,*
machine quilted by Wanda Rains (51" × 51").

*Here is a rather contemporary-looking
take on the Straight Furrows setting.
There are 23 blocks with red **B4-C3-
D2** arcs and 13 with yellow. I cut all
the **A1** squares separately, positioning
them at the layout stage in a process
of trial and error until a satisfying
arrangement emerged. The variety
of black and white prints provides
interesting textures, and the wavy
border adds to the sense of skewed
irregularity.*

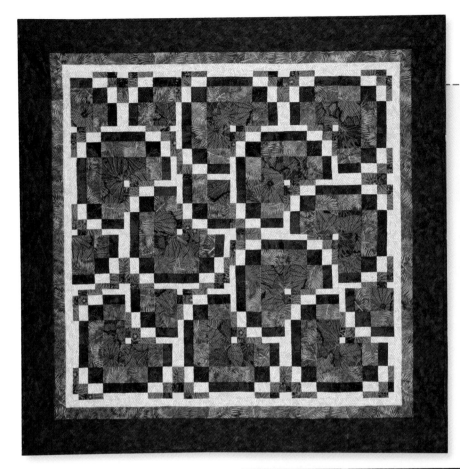

Forest Flowers *Pieced by Michelle Hoel, machine quilted by Lynne Turner-Liro (55½" × 55½").*

*Forest Flowers is a creative asymmetrical arrangement of the Card Trick setting. All 36 blocks are the same; golden connecting **A4-B3-C2-D1** arcs create intricate pathways leading the eye around the quilt. The colors are rich and summery. It reminds me of a forest I visited in Mongolia, where there were patches of gorgeous wild peonies with large dark pink blooms, and dappled sunlight filtered through the trees.*

Floral Tropicana *Made by Lisa Jenni (51" × 51").*

*In this stunning quilt, the Card Trick setting is placed in a Trip Around the World setting. The two multicolored bird of paradise fabrics of differing print scales are featured beautifully in the blocks and the border. There are three block types: 12 central blocks in the Card Trick; 12 blocks with orange **A1** squares and black bird of paradise fabric surrounding the center; and 12 corner blocks with fussy-cut floral **A1** squares. The piecing extends into the bird of paradise borders, making a pleasing resolution to the pattern.*

Easter Morning   *Pieced by the author, machine quilted by Wanda Rains (55" × 55").*

Spring bursts forth on Easter Morning. There are three block types: 16 orange, 12 teal and eight cream. The sashing strips separate the confluence of **A1** squares and add to the overall pattern. Notice the secondary pattern that crosses the boundaries of the teal and cream blocks.

Safari Quilt   *Pieced by Marilyn Ahnemiller, machine quilted by Cindy Gilbrough (60" × 60").*

The 36 blocks are all the same and grouped into nine mega-blocks, with the small **D4** squares coming together at the centers. It looks like a giant nine-patch, with the triple sashing highlighting the mega-blocks. The wonderful pieced border of skinny triangles provides a contrast to the squares and greatly enhances the center field. Safari Quilt is a fitting title for this piece with vibrant colors and an African atmosphere.

Wolf Reflections   *Made by Wanda Rains (67" × 67").*

Use the Bargello blocks to make an attractive setting for a pictorial panel. The panel replaces the four center blocks, which have migrated to the corners where they are cornerstones for the wide border. All 36 blocks are the same; the setting with sashing is similar to the project quilt Reflections (page 82). Wanda Rains made this quilt for her 10-year-old great-nephew, Christian, after he informed her that he wanted a wolf quilt.

chapter 5

BARGELLO BLOCKS ON POINT

Setting the Bargello blocks on-point gives them an entirely new look. In this format with the inclusion of setting triangles, an on-point quilt with 24 blocks is approximately the same size as a 36-blocker set squarely (such as the projects in Chapter Four). This is a great way to increase the size of your quilt without making more blocks.

The project and Gallery quilts illustrate some of the many possible variations. The simplest project is made from 24 blocks of one type. As we progress to several block types and add sashing, the patterns look more complex and sophisticated.

The medallion-style project is so named after traditional medallion quilts in which there is a central pattern with borders added. In the Four-Patch setting, the four large **A1** squares come together in adjacent blocks so that the four-patch is clearly visible. Once again, the addition of sashing adds a whole new dimension to the design.

Bainbridge Delft Pieced by the author, machine quilted by Wanda Rains (51" × 51").

Bainbridge Delft: 24-Block Quilt

QUILT SIZE: 51" × 51" • BLOCK SIZE: 7"

MATERIALS LIST

- 2 yards dark floral for blocks, setting triangles, outer border and binding
- ½ yard blue floral for blocks and middle border
- 1⅓ yards white/blue floral for blocks and inner border
- ⅓ yard periwinkle dot for blocks

- ½ yard white for blocks
- ¼ yard light blue floral for blocks
- ¼ yard dark blue mono for blocks
- 55" × 55" batting
- 55" × 55" backing fabric

This classic blue and white quilt would make an attractive wall hanging or lap quilt. The white gives the pattern clarity. In combination with the delicate blue floral prints, it reminds me of fine English bone china or Delft pottery.

The quilt has 24 blocks all of the same type set, with large setting triangles and a triple mitered border. It's a good starter project, using only one block type in a simple setting.

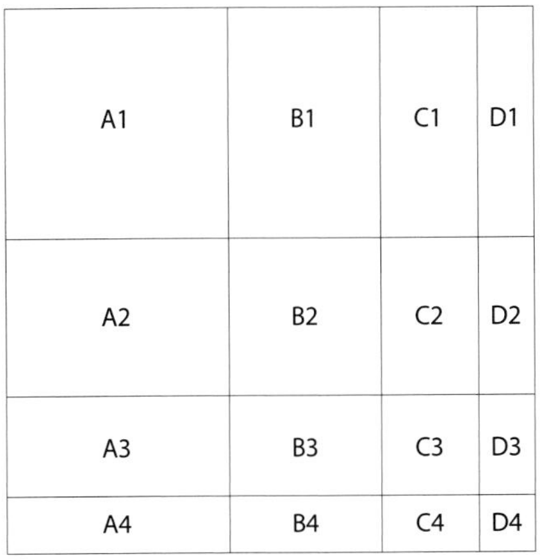

A1	B1	C1	D1
A2	B2	C2	D2
A3	B3	C3	D3
A4	B4	C4	D4

Bargello Block Diagram

Constructing Bainbridge Delft

1. Piece the 24 blocks as instructed in Chapter Two. You should have 3 **A** strip sets, 2 **B** strip sets and 1 each of **C** and **D** before you make the counter-cuts. Counter-cut the **A** sets 3½", the **B** sets 2½", the **C** set 1¾" and the **D** set 1¼": 24 segments of each. The **C** set will yield only 22 segments; you need 24. Use leftovers of the **D** strip set to make the final 2 **C** segments (see page 40). Join the segments to complete the blocks.

2. First cut the 4 outer border strips (54" × 3") lengthwise from the dark floral fabric. Next cut four 12" squares for the setting and corner triangles. Divide 2 into quarters by cutting diagonally both ways for the 8 setting triangles. Cut the other 2 in half diagonally for the corner triangles. Lay out the blocks in the desired configuration with the setting and corner triangles; use the photograph as a guide or make your own pattern.

3. Assemble the center field of the quilt, joining the components in diagonal rows (see page 46). Trim away the excess from the sides, leaving ¼" seam allowances all the way around (see page 47).

4. You should already have the inner and outer border strips cut (see Step 2). Cut and join 5 full-width 1¼" strips for the middle blue floral borders to make 4 (50" × 1¼"). Strip piece the inner, middle and outer border strips; join them to the quilt top, mitering the corners (see page 48). Alternatively, add each border in turn, joining the sides first, then the tops and bottoms (see page 48).

5. Baste, quilt and bind as directed in Chapter One. Binding strips may be cut lengthwise from the dark floral. Bainbridge Delft has an overall floral quilting pattern.

Bainbridge Delft Block
Required: 24 blocks.

CUTTING FOR 24 BLOCKS

Note: Cut strips across the full width of the fabric, selvage to selvage (40"), except for white/blue floral.

White/blue floral: First cut 4 border strips (2¼" × 48") lengthwise, then cut strips for blocks lengthwise.

Fabric	Block Part	No. of Strips	Size
Dark Floral	A1	3	3½" × 40"
White/Blue Floral	A2	3	2½" × 40"
	B1	2	3½" × 40"
Periwinkle Dot	A3	3	1¾" × 40"
	C1	1	3½" × 40"
Blue Floral	B2	2	2½" × 40"
	C3	1	1¾" × 40"
	D4	1	1¼" × 40"
White	A4	3	1¼" × 40"
	B3	2	1¾" × 40"
	C2	1	2½" × 40"
	D1	1	3½" × 40"
Dark Blue Mono	B4	2	1¼" × 40"
	D2	1	2½" × 40"
Light Blue	C4	1	1¼" × 40"
	D3	1	1¾" × 40"

Gothic Medallion Pieced by the author, machine quilted by Wanda Rains (49" × 49").

Gothic Medallion: 24-Block Quilt

MEDALLION SETTING • QUILT SIZE: 49" × 49" • BLOCK SIZE: 7"

MATERIALS LIST

- 1½ yards large print for blocks, setting triangles and borders (allows for fussy-cutting)
- ½ yard turquoise for blocks, setting triangles and borders
- ½ yard green for blocks and borders
- 1 yard black for blocks and binding
- 1¼ yards purple tonal for blocks, setting triangles and borders

- ¼ yard purple floral for blocks
- ¼ yard light/multiwave for blocks
- 54" × 54" batting
- 54" × 54" backing fabric

This is a mysterious, dark and handsome quilt with brilliant highlights that accentuate the emerging secondary patterns. It was inspired by the large multicolored print, fussy-cut to create an additional dynamic layer of patterns and complexity. The fussy-cutting, pieced borders and setting triangles make this a more challenging project; attention to detail with accuracy is essential.

Like Bainbridge Delft (see page 92), Gothic Medallion is constructed from 24 blocks, but there are two block types. The block types are exactly the same apart from the **A2** and **B1** pieces. In 16 blocks these are turquoise; in eight they are green.

Another difference is that the setting triangles are pieced so that the two little side-by-side turquoise squares that appear toward the center of the quilt are mirrored at the sides. I've also fussy-cut small pieces to interrupt the inner border strip, and the borders have cornerstones.

A1	B1	C1	D1
A2	B2	C2	D2
A3	B3	C3	D3
A4	B4	C4	D4

Bargello Block Diagram

Fussy-Cut A1 Squares Come Together *They create a large decorative square at the center of the quilt.*

Constructing Gothic Medallion
(See the cutting charts on pages 98-99.)

1. Piece the 24 blocks as instructed in Chapter Two. There are 16 blocks with turquoise **A2** and **B1** patches, and 8 with green **A2** and **B1**. Make 2 of the **A** sets with turquoise strips and the third with a green strip. Make 1 of the **B** sets with turquoise and the other with green. The **C** and **D** strip sets are the same for both the turquoise and green block types. Counter-cut the **A** sets 3½" and the **B** sets 2½": 16 segments with turquoise and 8 segments with green of each. Counter-cut the **C** set 1¾" and the **D** set 1¼": 24 segments of each. The **C** set will yield only 22 segments; you need 24. Use leftovers of the **D** strip set to make the final 2 segments (see page 40). Join the segments to complete the blocks. If you would like to play with the orientation and placement of the fussy-cut **A1** squares, piece the blocks in sections until you have worked out the desired configuration (see page 39).

2. For the setting and corner triangles, you may manipulate the fabric and fussy-cut for particular sections of the large print. Cut two 9½" squares diagonally both ways into quarters for the 8 setting triangles, and two 11½" squares diagonally one way into halves for the 4 corner triangles. The setting and corners triangles also contain purple and turquoise pieces. From the turquoise, cut 8 squares (1¼") and 4 rectangles (2" × 1¼"). From the purple tonal, cut 24 strips (8" × 1¼") from 5 full-width 1¼" strips.

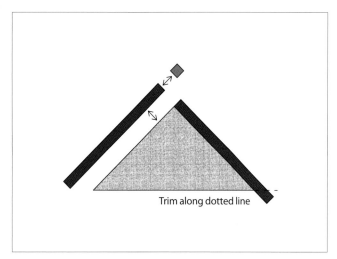

Diagram of Setting Triangle *Sew strip to triangle. Sew square to strip, then join onto triangle. Trim away excess strips in line with long side of the triangle.*

Close-Up of Corner Triangle

Close-Up of Setting Triangle

3. Construct the 8 setting triangles. Sew 1 purple strip onto a short side of each of the small triangles. Align the pieces at the 90-degree corner of the triangle and stitch toward the point. Your strips will be longer than the triangle edge. Press the seams open. Join 1 turquoise square onto each of 8 purple strips. Press the seams open, then attach to the other short side of the triangle, aligning the 90-degree corner as before. Press the seams open. Trim away the excess strips flush with the long edge of the triangle. (See diagram above.)

4. Construct the 4 corner triangles. You should have 8 remaining purple strips. Sew these in pairs with turquoise rectangles in between. Attach the pieced strips to the long side of the large fussy-cut triangles, being sure to center them accurately. Trim the excess strips away, flush with the triangle.

5. Lay out the blocks in the desired configuration with the setting and corner triangles; use the photograph as a guide or make your own pattern. Assemble the center field of the quilt, joining the components in diagonal rows (see page 46). Trim away the excess from the sides, leaving ¼" seam allowances all the way around (see page 47).

Close-Up of Center Side of Border

Close-Up of Pieced Cornerstones

6. Cut the pieces for the borders (see page 99). Join the 8 inner purple strips to the 8 middle green strips. Sew these together in pairs with the fussy-cut 2½" × 2½" squares in between. Measure the center field of the quilt across its middle. It should measure approximately 39-41". Trim the 4 pieced borders to the same length, making sure that the fussy-cut squares are centered. Trim the outer purple border strips to the same length and stitch them adjacent to the green strips.

7. Make the 4 pieced cornerstones. Sew the 4 turquoise squares onto 4 of the purple strips and press the seams toward the strip. Attach 1 each of the remaining 4 strips to the 4 fussy-cut 4" × 4" squares and press the seams toward the strips. Join the 4 strips with squares onto these. Take care to maintain the desired orientation of the fussy-cut pieces when adding the strips.

8. Attach the side borders to the center field. Join the cornerstones to each end of the pieced top and bottom borders, being careful to maintain the correct orientation. Attach them to the quilt top.

9. Baste, quilt and bind as directed in Chapter One. The quilt has an overall quilting pattern of feathers or plumes in an attractive variegated thread.

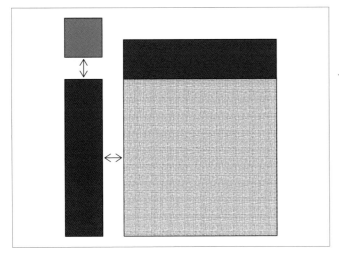

Construction of Pieced Cornerstone   *Join a strip to the fussy-cut corner square. Next join a strip to the small turquoise square, then to the corner square.*

Turquoise Block
Required: 16 blocks.

Green Block
Required: 8 blocks.

CUTTING FOR 24 BLOCKS

Note: Cut strips across the full width of the fabric, selvage to selvage (40").

*Option for **A1** squares: Fussy-cut the 24 squares 3½".*

Fabric	Block Part	No. of Strips	Size
Large Print*	**A1**	3	3½" × 40"
Green	**A2**	1	2½" × 40"
	B1	1	3½" × 40"
Turquoise	**A2**	2	2½" × 40"
	B1	1	3½" × 40"
	D4	1	1¼" × 40"
Purple Tonal	**A3**	3	1¾" × 40"
	B2	2	2½" × 40"
	C1	1	3½" × 40"
Black	**A4**	3	1¼" × 40"
	B3	2	1¾" × 40"
	C2	1	2½" × 40"
	D1	1	3½" × 40"
Light/ Multiwave	**B4**	2	1¼" × 40"
	C3	1	1¾" × 40"
	D2	1	2½" × 40"
Purple Floral	**C4**	1	1¼" × 40"
	D3	1	1¾" × 40"

TAKING THE PRESSURE OUT OF QUILTING

Be realistic about your skill level and the time available to complete the project.

Setting goals and deadlines provides good incentives, but be a little flexible so that you can enjoy making the quilt without feeling pressured.

CUTTING FOR BORDERS

Border Part	Fabric	Number	Size
Border Center Squares	Large Print	4 Fussy-Cut	2½" × 2½"
Border Cornerstones	Large Print	4 Fussy-Cut	4" × 4"
Border Baby Cornerstones	Turquoise	4	1¼" × 1¼"
Border Corners	Purple Tonal	8	1¼" × 4"
Inner Border Strips	Purple Tonal	8	1¼" × 20"
Middle Border Strips	Green	8	1¾" × 20"
Outer Border Strips	Purple Tonal	4	2¾" × full width selvage to selvage

American Hero's Bargello: 40-Block Quilt

FOUR-PATCH SETTING • QUILT SIZE: 62" × 62" • BLOCK SIZE: 7"

MATERIALS LIST

- 2 yards red large print for blocks, setting triangles and borders
- 1¼ yards cream for blocks
- ½ yard blue bunnies for blocks
- ½ yard red mono for blocks and cornerstones
- ⅓ yard blue large print for blocks
- ½ yard beige with red stars for blocks

- ⅔ yard blue with beige stars for blocks and cornerstones
- ½ yard multistars for border
- ⅔ yard blue for binding
- 66½" × 66½" batting
- 66½" × 66½" backing fabric

This patriotic red, white and blue lap quilt makes an excellent decorative accent for special holidays or throughout the year. The blue and red large squares come together to form four-patches, attractively framed by the cream fabric. An American veteran will be honored with this quilt as a gift through the American Hero's Quilt Donor Program.

This quilt has a total of 40 blocks—20 each of two block types. The positioning of the cream fabric is the same in both sets of blocks, so it forms frames around the four-patches and a more intricate pattern in the area where the small **D4** squares come together.

Arcs of red mono fabric in the **A4-B3-C2-D1** patches of the red blocks link the blocks forming red waves running through the quilt design. The red large print in the setting triangles and border is a wonderful background for floating the blocks.

A1	B1	C1	D1
A2	B2	C2	D2
A3	B3	C3	D3
A4	B4	C4	D4

Bargello block diagram

Constructing American Hero's Bargello
(See the cutting charts on page 102.)

1. Piece the 40 blocks as instructed in Chapter Two: 20 of the red type and 20 of the blue type. You should have 2 **A** and **B** strip sets, and 1 each of **C** and **D** for each block type before you make the counter-cuts. Counter-cut the **A** sets 3½", the **B** sets 2½", the **C** set 1¾" and the **D** set 1¼": 20 segments of each for both block types. Join the segments to complete the blocks.

2. From 60" of the red large print fabric, cut 4 outer border strips (5" × 60") and five 12" squares lengthwise from the fabric. Divide 3 of the squares into quarters by cutting diagonally both ways for the 12 setting triangles. Cut the other 2 in half diagonally for the corner triangles. Lay out the blocks in the desired configuration with the setting and corner triangles; use the photograph as a guide or make your own pattern.

3. Assemble the center field of the quilt, joining the components in diagonal rows (see page 46). Trim away the excess from the sides, leaving ¼" seam allowances all the way around (see page 47). The completed center field should measure 50" × 50" across the center. If the measurement is different, adjust the length of the border strips accordingly (see page 48).

4. Cut 5 full-width 2" strips and piece them to make 4 inner border strips (50" × 2") from the multistars fabric. Cut 4 cornerstones (2" × 2") from the red mono fabric. Trim the outer border strips to 53" and cut the 4 cornerstones (5" × 5") from the blue with beige stars fabric. Add each border in turn, joining the sides first, then the tops and bottoms with cornerstones attached (see page 48). Check your quilt top dimensions after adding each border and before cutting the next.

5. Baste, quilt and bind as directed in Chapter One. The American Hero's Bargello quilt has an overall quilting pattern of loops and swirls. The back of the quilt is made from leftovers of strip sets and odd pieces of fabric (see photograph on page 103).

A1 Red Block
Required: 20 blocks.

A1 Blue Block
Required: 20 blocks.

CUTTING FOR 20 RED BLOCKS

Note: Cut strips across the full width of the fabric, selvage to selvage (40").

Fabric	Block Part	No. of Strips	Size
Red Large Print	A1	2	3½" × 40"
Cream	A2	2	2½" × 40"
	B1	2	3½" × 40"
	B4	2	1¼" × 40"
	C3	1	1¾" × 40"
	D2	1	2½" × 40"
Blue Bunnies	A3	2	1¾" × 40"
	B2	2	2½" × 40"
	C1	1	3½" × 40"
	C4	1	1¼" × 40"
	D3	1	1¾" × 40"
Red Mono	A4	2	1¼" × 40"
	B3	2	1¾" × 40"
	C2	1	2½" × 40"
	D1	1	3½" × 40"
	D4	1	1¼" × 40"

CUTTING FOR 20 BLUE BLOCKS

Note: Cut strips across the full width of the fabric, selvage to selvage (40").

Fabric	Block Part	No. of Strips	Size
Blue Large Print	A1	2	3½" × 40"
Cream	A2	2	2½" × 40"
	B1	2	3½" × 40"
	B4	2	1¼" × 40"
	C3	1	1¾" × 40"
	D2	1	2½" × 40"
	D4	1	1¼" × 40"
Beige with Red Stars	A3	2	1¾" × 40"
	B2	2	2½" × 40"
	C1	1	3½" × 40"
	C4	1	1¼" × 40"
	D3	1	1¾" × 40"
Blue with Beige Stars	A4	2	1¼" × 40"
	B3	2	1¾" × 40"
	C2	1	2½" × 40"
	D1	1	3½" × 40"

Pieced Back of Quilt   *The back of American Hero's Bargello shows pieced leftover sections of strip sets and odd pieces of fabric.*

Savannah Sunrise Pieced by the author, machine quilted by Wanda Rains (70" × 58½").

Savannah Sunrise: *32-Block Quilt*

WITH SASHING • QUILT SIZE: 70" × 58½" • BLOCK SIZE: 7"

MATERIALS LIST

- ¼ yard lime green circles for blocks and cornerstones
- 2¼ yards black with white dots for blocks and borders
- ½ yard black and white lines for blocks and cornerstones
- ½ yard dark multidots for blocks
- ½ yard orange bubbles for blocks
- ⅛ yard yellow for blocks
- 1¾ yards orange stripe for blocks, setting triangles and binding
- ⅓ yard leopard spots for blocks and cornerstones

- ½ yard pale multispots for blocks
- ½ yard red with white dots for blocks and cornerstones
- ½ yard blue/lime green stripe for blocks and cornerstones (option: 1 yard to cut strips on bias)
- ⅔ yard dark brown woven for sashing
- ½ yard black with gray swirls for sashing
- 76" × 64" batting
- 76" × 64" backing fabric

This large lap quilt or wall hanging with an African feel will bring color and warmth wherever it goes. Enjoy using unusual prints to create this vibrant piece. The addition of sashing separates and highlights the blocks, which would be too busy if they were set side by side. Cornerstone fabrics are carefully selected to link the blocks, making secondary patterns emerge.

Savannah Sunrise has 32 Bargello blocks. There are two block types: 20 of one and 12 of the other. The block types alternate in horizontal rows and are enclosed by brown and black sashing strips. They shimmer on the hot orange setting triangles. The use of leftovers from the strip sets in the border brings all the colors out to the boundaries, adding unity and closure to the design.

The block orientation is the same one used in Purple Passion (page 111). Notice what a difference adding sashing makes.

A1	B1	C1	D1
A2	B2	C2	D2
A3	B3	C3	D3
A4	B4	C4	D4

Bargello Block Diagram

Constructing Savannah Sunrise

(See the cutting charts on page 106.)

1. Piece the 32 blocks as instructed in Chapter Two. For the 12 black and white blocks, you should have 1 of each strip set. The **A** set will yield only 11 segments; you need 12. Use leftovers of the **B** strip set to make the 12th segment (see page 40). For the 20 red multi-dot blocks, you should have 2 **A** and **B** strip sets and 1 each of **C** and **D** before you make the counter-cuts. Counter-cut the **A** sets 3½", the **B** sets 2½", the **C** set 1¾" and the **D** set 1¼": 12 segments of each for the black and white blocks and 20 segments of each for the red multidot blocks. Join the segments to complete the blocks.

2. Cut four 15" squares and two 9" squares from the orange striped fabric. Divide the 15" squares into quarters, cutting them diagonally both ways for the 14 setting triangles (you will have 2 extras). Cut the 9" squares in half diagonally one way for the 4 corner triangles. Cut the 80 sashing strips (1¾" × 7½"), 32 black and 48 brown; and the 49 cornerstones (1¾" × 1¾"), 22 lime green circles, 8 black and white line, 8 leopard spots, 7 red with white dots and 4 blue/lime green stripes. (**Option:** Cut on bias so stripes are vertical.)

3. Lay out the blocks in the desired configuration with the sashing, cornerstones, setting and corner triangles; use the photograph as a guide or make your own pattern. If you use a striped fabric for the setting triangles, be aware of the direction of the stripe. Assemble the center field of the quilt, joining the components in diagonal rows (see page 46). Trim away the excess from the sides, leaving ¼" seam allowances all the way around (see page 47).

4. Measure the center field across the middle. It should measure approximately 60" × 48½". If your measurement is different, you will need to make adjustments. Check the measurements of the quilt top at every step and change the length of the border strips as necessary (see page 48). Cut border strips from the black and white dots fabric lengthwise. Inner border: 2 sides (60" × 1¼"), top and bottom (50" × 1¼"). Outer border: 2 sides (64" × 3½"), top and bottom (58½" × 3½"). The middle border is made by cutting 1¾" segments from the leftover strip sets and joining these into two 61½" strips for the sides and two 52½" strips for the top and bottom. Join each border in turn, first sewing the sides, then the top and bottom (see page 48).

5. Baste, quilt and bind as directed in Chapter One. Savannah Sunrise has an overall quilting pattern of bubbles in assorted sizes stitched in variegated thread.

Black and White Block
Required: 12 blocks.

Red Multidot Block
Required: 20 blocks.

CUTTING FOR 12 BLACK AND WHITE BLOCKS

Note: Cut strips across the full width of the fabric, selvage to selvage (40").

Fabric	Block Part	No. of Strips	Size
Lime Green Circles	A1	1	3½" × 40"
Black with White Dots	A2	1	2½" × 40"
	B1	1	3½" × 40"
Black and White Lines	A3	1	1¾" × 40"
	B2	1	2½" × 40"
	C1	1	3½" × 40"
Dark Multidots	A4	1	1¼" × 40"
	B3	1	1¾" × 40"
	C2	1	2½" × 40"
	D1	1	3½" × 40"
Orange Bubbles	B4	1	1¼" × 40"
	C3	1	1¾" × 40"
	D2	1	2½" × 40"
Orange Stripe	C4	1	1¼" × 40"
	D3	1	1¾" × 40"
Yellow	D4	1	1¼" × 40"

CUTTING FOR 20 RED MULTIDOT BLOCKS

Note: Cut strips across the full width of the fabric, selvage to selvage (40").

Option for blue/lime green stripe: Cut strips on the bias so that stripe orientation in the block is vertical.

Fabric	Block Part	No. of Strips	Size
Leopard Spots	A1	2	3½" × 40"
Pale Multispots	A2	2	2½" × 40"
	B1	2	3½" × 40"
Red with White Dots	A3	2	1¾" × 40"
	B2	2	2½" × 40"
	C1	1	3½" × 40"
Blue/Lime Green Stripe*	A4	2	1¼" × 40"
	B3	2	1¾" × 40"
	C2	1	2½" × 40"
	D1	1	3½" × 40"
Orange Bubbles	B4	2	1¼" × 40"
	C3	1	1¾" × 40"
	D2	1	2½" × 40"
Orange Stripe	C4	1	1¼" × 40"
	D3	1	1¾" × 40"
Yellow	D4	1	1¼" × 40"

FOR VERTICAL STRIPES

On my quilt, the direction of the blue/lime green stripes is vertical. To achieve this, I cut the strips on the bias and had to piece the blocks in reverse order, i.e., place the **A** segment on top of the **B** and the **C** segment on top of the **D** (instead of vice versa). You may like to experiment to create the look you want.

Detail of Border

GALLERY

Swimming in Circles   *Pieced by Joanne Bennett, machine quilted by Wanda Rains (50½" × 50½").*

*This quilt is the same layout as Bainbridge Delft (page 92), apart from the center four blocks which are turned so that the **A1** squares come together like those in Gothic Medallion (page 94). The blocks are all alike except for the **A1** squares. There are ten fishy **A1** squares fussy-cut and oriented so that they swim around in a circle.*

Gecko Madness   *Pieced by Anita Webb, machine quilted by Deb Lund (96" × 96").*

*The 36 blocks (20 green and 16 orange) in this medallion-style bed quilt look stunning set on the large black background. Notice the creative use of the orange sashing around the central 16 blocks and the leftover **C** strip sets from the orange blocks on the sides.*

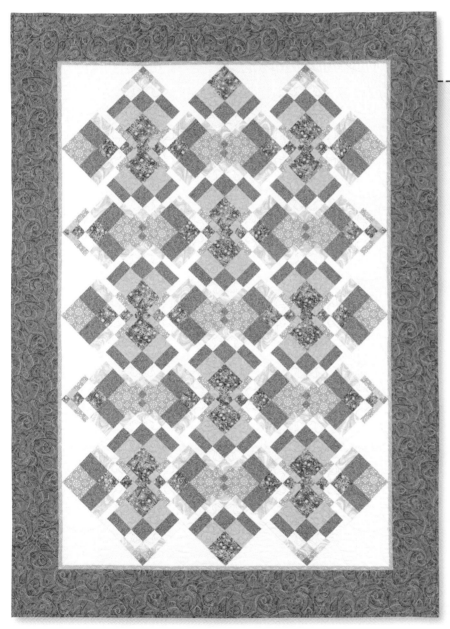

Summer Lime   *Pieced by Penny J. Evers,
machine quilted by Cindy Paulsgrove
(71" × 52").*

Summer Lime has 38 blocks (two types:
20 and 18), arranged in the Tessellated Butterfly setting. Compare this
on-point version to the squarely set
quilts of the same setting (for example,
Bedtime Butterflies on page 65). The
light lemon side triangles, beautifully
quilted, provide a perfect background
to float the blocks.

109

Twist of Glitz *Made by Klina Dupuy (64" × 46").*

*This quilt really sparkles from the unusual hand-painted and metallic printed fabrics. There are two block types: 16 with pink and 20 with black **A4-B3-C2-D1** arcs, grouped into eight heart mega-blocks and six singles on the sides. Once again, the sashing separates these bright and bold blocks and is an integral part of the overall design.*

Purple Passion *Pieced by Carol McKim, machine quilted by Wanda Rains (47" × 46").*

The 25 blocks are all set the same way, creating a striking zigzag effect across the quilt. The purple makes a rich background to highlight the blocks. Compare this with Savannah Sunrise (page 104), which has two block types set in the same way, but with sashing.

Zigzag Zinnias, aka The Garden Is Coming to Get You! *Pieced by the author, machine quilted by Wanda Rains (63" × 52½").*

What began as a project quilt with 32 blocks rapidly became rather complex. I was having great fun designing using an Electric Quilt® program on the computer. As the pattern became more sophisticated, two of the five block types broke the basic symmetry rule (**A2** and **B1** fabrics are different). Originally I wasn't planning to include sashing strips; but the blocks all merged together, so I grouped them into mega-blocks and added the black strips to separate them. This intensified the colors and enhanced the design.

chapter 6

MORE AND MORE BLOCKS

With more and more Bargello blocks added to the quilt, the scope for increasing the complexity of the design continues to grow. You could stick to a simple pattern and make the quilt larger; Field of Flowers (page 114) is an expanded version of Autumn Harvest, the Straight Furrows project in Chapter Four.

At the other extreme, Heart of the Arctic (photo opposite and page 124) contains nine different block types. If you'd like to experiment and create sophisticated patterns, I recommend the aid of computer software such as Electric Quilt®.

Blocks may be clustered into groups of four to create mega-blocks, as in Rebel (page 118) Use these mega-blocks to generate more pattern possibilities. In Rebel, they are oriented to give the look of a tiled floor, with skinny sashing that looks like grouting.

Again, you have the opportunity to design your own unique quilt.

Field of Flowers Pieced by Pam Syracuse, machine quilted by Kim McBride, ANG Quilting (68" × 68").

Field of Flowers: 64-Block Quilt

STRAIGHT FURROWS SETTING • **QUILT SIZE: 68" × 68"** • **BLOCK SIZE: 7"**

MATERIALS LIST

- 2½ yards floral theme for block and borders
- ½ yard lime floral for blocks
- ⅔ yard blue butterflies for blocks
- 1⅔ yards red for blocks, borders and binding
- ¼ yard pink for blocks
- ½ yard orange for blocks
- ⅔ yard gold for blocks
- ⅔ yard purple for blocks
- ¼ yard blue for blocks
- 72" × 72" batting
- 72" × 72" backing fabric

Brighten up your couch and bring the garden indoors with this large floral lap quilt, which is quick and simple to piece. Warm waves of color draw the eye across the surface of the Straight Furrows setting. Choose an attractive floral theme fabric to provide the source of all the pretty hues in the companion fabrics.

Field of Flowers has two block types, with 32 blocks of each type. The floral theme fabric appears in the **A1** large square and in the **B4-C3-D2** arc in both types. This helps to unify and link the blocks, creating flowing lines.

Notice how different this quilt looks from Autumn Harvest (see page 78), the 36-block Straight Furrows project quilt, in which the large **A1** squares are accentuated.

A1	B1	C1	D1
A2	B2	C2	D2
A3	B3	C3	D3
A4	B4	C4	D4

Bargello Block Diagram

Constructing Field of Flowers

(See the cutting charts on page 116.)

1. **Option:** Before cutting the floral theme strips for the blocks, cut the 4 long outer border strips (70" × 4¾") lengthwise from the fabric. Then cut the strips for the blocks lengthwise, too. If you don't mind joining the border strips, proceed with cutting the full-width strips for the blocks in the usual way from selvage to selvage.

2. Piece the 2 types of blocks: 32 red and 32 purple, as directed in Chapter Two. You should have 3 **A** strip sets, 2 **B** and **C** strips sets and 1 **D** set for each block type. Counter-cut the **A** sets 3½", the **B** sets 2½", the **C** sets 1¾" and the **D** set 1¼": 32 segments of each for both block types. Join the segments to complete the blocks.

3. Lay out the blocks in the desired configuration; use the photograph as a guide or make your own pattern. Assemble the center field of the quilt, joining the blocks in rows (see page 46). It should measure 56½" × 56½" across the center. If the measurement is different, change the length of the border strips accordingly (see page 48).

4. Cut 8 full-width 2" red strips for the inner border. Join them in pairs; trim 2 to 56½" × 2" for the sides of the quilt and 2 to 59½" × 2" for the top and bottom. Cut 8 full-width 4¾" strips of theme fabric for the outer border and join them in pairs (unless you already cut them lengthwise for the **Option** in Step 1). Trim 2 to 59½" × 4¾" for the sides and 2 to 68" × 4¾" for the top and bottom. Add each border in turn; first the sides, then the top and bottom. Check the measurements of the quilt top at every step and adjust as necessary (see page 48). Alternatively, sew the inner and outer border strips together before trimming, then attach to the quilt top and miter the corners (see page 48).

5. Baste, quilt and bind as directed in Chapter One. Field of Flowers has an allover quilting pattern of butterflies and flowers.

Red Block
Required: 32 blocks.

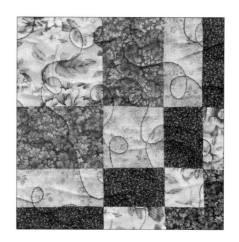

Purple Block
Required: 32 blocks.

CUTTING FOR 32 RED BLOCKS

Note: Cut strips across the full width of the fabric, selvage to selvage (40").

D3 and **D4** are combined into one strip.

Fabric	Block Part	No. of Strips	Size
Floral Theme	**A1**	3	3½" × 40"
	B4	2	1¼" × 40"
	C3	2	1¾" × 40"
	D2	1	2½" × 40"
Lime Floral	**A2**	3	2½" × 40"
	B1	2	3½" × 40"
Blue Butterflies	**A3**	3	1¾" × 40"
	B2	2	2½" × 40"
	C1	2	3½" × 40"
Red	**A4**	3	1¼" × 40"
	B3	2	1¾" × 40"
	C2	2	2½" × 40"
	D1	1	3½" × 40"
Pink	**C4**	2	1¼" × 40"
	D3 /D4	1	2½" × 40"

CUTTING FOR 32 PURPLE BLOCKS

Note: Cut strips across the full width of the fabric, selvage to selvage (40").

D3 and **D4** are combined into one strip.

Fabric	Block Part	No. of Strips	Size
Floral Theme	**A1**	3	3½" × 40"
	B4	2	1¼" × 40"
	C3	2	1¾" × 40"
	D2	1	2½" × 40"
Orange	**A2**	3	2½" × 40"
	B1	2	3½" × 40"
Gold	**A3**	3	1¾" × 40"
	B2	2	2½" × 40"
	C1	2	3½" × 40"
Purple	**A4**	3	1¼" × 40"
	B3	2	1¾" × 40"
	C2	2	2½" × 40"
	D1	1	3½" × 40"
Blue	**C4**	2	1¼" × 40"
	D3/ D4	1	2½" × 40"

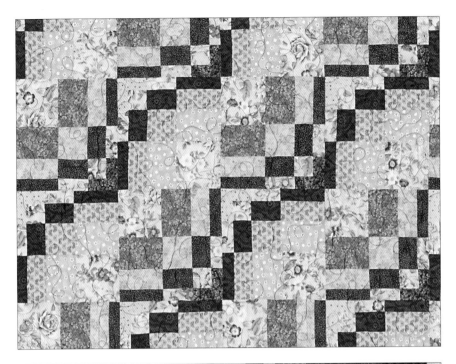

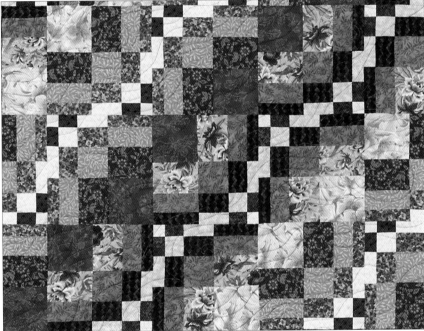

Details of Field of Flowers (top) and Autumn Harvest (bottom) *With their strong diagonal flow, the quilts demonstrate the different results that can be achieved with Bargello blocks in the Straight Furrows setting.*

Rebel Pieced by the author, machine quilted by Wanda Rains (81" × 66½"). Fabric from the "Rebel" line by David Textiles Inc., designed by the author and Beth Bruske. Photo by Mark Frey.

Rebel: Mega-Block Quilt

TILED FLOOR SETTING • QUILT SIZE: 81" × 66½" • BLOCK SIZE: 7"

MATERIALS LIST

- ½ yard khaki dragons for blocks and cornerstones
- 1½ yards cream barbed wire for blocks
- 1½ yards black for blocks, sashing strips and borders
- ½ yard red fire for blocks
- ½ yard khaki dragons and flames for blocks
- 1½ yards gray barbed wire for blocks
- 1 yard red dragons and flames for blocks and cornerstones

- ½ yard khaki fire for blocks
- ½ yard red tattoo for blocks and cornerstones
- 2¼ yards khaki tattoo for borders and binding
- 85" × 69" batting
- 85" × 69" backing fabric

Create mega-blocks and add narrow sashing for this handsome, undoubtedly masculine-looking quilt in the Tiled Floor setting. The majestic secondary patterns that emerge across the "grouting" make the quilt look complex and intricate.

Notice how the red squares on the diagonals form their own pattern, linking the blocks and adding another dimension to this exciting design. This was my first Bargello block quilt, which sowed the seeds for this book.

The 80 blocks are arranged in 20 mega-blocks (clusters of four) separated by narrow sashing strips. The 64-piece mega-block was originally designed as a single block. However, it's simpler to break it down into its four component block types and use the same piecing techniques as for the other quilts in this book.

There are two similar block types with bold black **A3-B2-C1** arcs. The other two block types both feature the gray barbed wire fabric. The latter differ only in the positioning of the two khaki fabrics, which are reversed so that one block type is a mirror image of the other. Note that the gray blocks are not exactly symmetrical on either side of the **A1, B2, C3** and **D4** diagonal because of the use of the two different khaki fabrics.

Bargello Block Diagram

A1	B1	C1	D1
A2	B2	C2	D2
A3	B3	C3	D3
A4	B4	C4	D4

Constructing Rebel
(See the cutting charts on pages 120-122.)

1. Piece 20 of each of the 4 block types, as instructed in Chapter Two. You should have 2 **A** and **B** strip sets and 1 each of the **C** and **D** strips sets for each block type. I recommend cutting and constructing each set separately before starting on the next, to minimize confusion. Counter-cut the **A** sets 3½", the **B** sets 2½", the **C** sets 1¾" and the **D** set 1¼": 20 segments of each for all the block types. Join the segments to complete the blocks for a total of 80 blocks.

2. Make the 20 mega-blocks. The mega-block consists of 4 blocks, 1 of each type. Join the blocks in pairs, then sew the pairs together in the configuration shown in the photograph on page 123. The mega-blocks should measure 14½" × 14½".

3. Cut 31 black sashing strips (1" × 14½"), 6 khaki dragon cornerstones (1" × 1") and 6 red dragons and flames cornerstones (1" × 1"). Lay out the blocks, sashing strips and cornerstones in the desired configuration; use the photograph as a guide or make your own pattern. Assemble the center field of the quilt, joining the components in rows (see page 46). The center field should measure 72½" × 58" across the center. If the measurement is different, change the length of the border strips accordingly (see page 48).

4. Cut the border pieces as indicated in the chart on page 122. Sew the black top and bottom strips to the khaki tattoo top and bottom panels and attach them to the quilt. Join the side sections in the following sequence: corner square, 4" black strip, 72½" side panel, 4" black strip, corner square. Attach them to 81" black side strips, and then to the quilt top. Use the diagram to help you with this piecing order.

5. Baste, quilt and bind as directed in Chapter One. Rebel has an allover diagonal quilting pattern of waves with curly whirlpools.

Khaki/Red Fire Block
Required: 20 blocks.

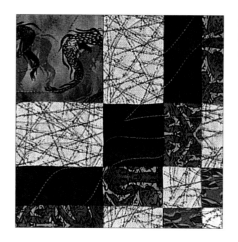

Khaki/Red Tattoo Block
Required: 20 blocks.

CUTTING FOR 20 KHAKI/RED FIRE BLOCKS

Note: Cut strips across the full width of the fabric, selvage to selvage (40").

Fabric	Block Part	No. of Strips	Size
Khaki Dragons	A1	2	3½" × 40"
Cream Barbed Wire	A2	2	2½" × 40"
	B1	2	3½" × 40"
	B4	2	1¼" × 40"
	C3	1	1¾" × 40"
	D2	1	2½" × 40"
Black	A3	2	1¾" × 40"
	B2	2	2½" × 40"
	C1	1	3½" × 40"
Red Fire	A4	2	1¼" × 40"
	B3	2	1¾" × 40"
	C2	2	2½" × 40"
	D1	1	3½" × 40"
Khaki Dragons and Flames	C4	1	1¼" × 40"
	D3	1	1¾" × 40"
Gray Barbed Wire	D4	1	1¼" × 40"

CUTTING FOR 20 KHAKI/RED TATTOO BLOCKS

Note: Cut strips across the full width of the fabric, selvage to selvage (40").

Fabric	Block Part	No. of Strips	Size
Khaki Dragons	A1	2	3½" × 40"
Cream Barbed Wire	A2	2	2½" × 40"
	B1	2	3½" × 40"
	B4	2	1¼" × 40"
	C3	1	1¾" × 40"
	D2	1	2½" × 40"
Black	A3	2	1¾" × 40"
	B2	2	2½" × 40"
	C1	1	3½" × 40"
Red Tattoo	A4	2	1¼" × 40"
	B3	2	1¾" × 40"
	C2	2	2½" × 40"
	D1	1	3½" × 40"
Khaki Dragons and Flames	C4	1	1¼" × 40"
	D3	1	1¾" × 40"
Gray Barbed Wire	D4	1	1¼" × 40"

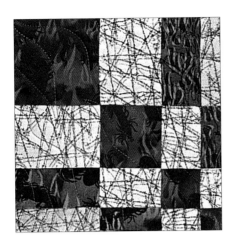

Gray Block
Required: 20 blocks.

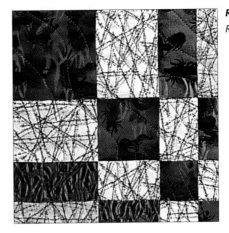

Reversed Gray Block
Required: 20 blocks.

CUTTING FOR 20 GRAY BLOCKS

Note: Cut strips across the full width of the fabric, selvage to selvage (40").

Fabric	Block Part	No. of Strips	Size
Red Dragons and Flames	A1	2	3½" × 40"
	B2	2	2½" × 40"
	C3	1	1¾" × 40"
	D4	1	1¼" × 40"
Gray Barbed Wire	A2	2	2½" × 40"
	B1	2	3½" × 40"
	B3	2	1¾" × 40"
	C2	1	2½" × 40"
	C4	1	1¼" × 40"
	D3	1	1¾" × 40"
Khaki Dragons and Flames	A3	2	1¾" × 40"
	B4	2	1¼" × 40"
Khaki Fire	C1	1	3½" × 40"
	D2	1	2½" × 40"
Cream Barbed Wire	A4	2	1¼" × 40"
	D1	1	3½" × 40"

CUTTING FOR 20 REVERSED GRAY BLOCKS

Note: Cut strips across the full width of the fabric, selvage to selvage (40").

Fabric	Block Part	No. of Strips	Size
Red Dragons and Flames	A1	2	3½" × 40"
	B2	2	2½" × 40"
	C3	1	1¾" × 40"
	D4	1	1¼" × 40"
Gray Barbed Wire	A2	2	2½" × 40"
	B1	2	3½" × 40"
	B3	2	1¾" × 40"
	C2	1	2½" × 40"
	C4	1	1¼" × 40"
	D3	1	1¾" × 40"
Khaki Fire	A3	2	1¾" × 40"
	B4	2	1¼" × 40"
Khaki Dragons and Flames	C1	1	3½" × 40"
	D2	1	2½" × 40"
Cream Barbed Wire	A4	2	1¼" × 40"
	D1	1	3½" × 40"

CUTTING FOR BORDERS

Border Part	Number	Size	Notes
Black strips top and bottom	2	1¼" × 58"	From joined strips
Black strips sides	2	1¼" × 81"	From joined strips
Black strips corners	4	1¼" × 4"	
Khaki tattoo top and bottom panels	2	4" × 58"	Cut lengthwise
Khaki tattoo side panels	2	4" × 72½"	Cut lengthwise
Red tattoo corner squares	4	4" × 4"	

DECISIONS, DECISIONS

If you are having trouble making decisions (such as on fabric choices or block arrangements), leave the project for a couple of hours. You will come back to it with a fresh perspective.

Rebel Mega-Block   *Photo by Mark Frey.*

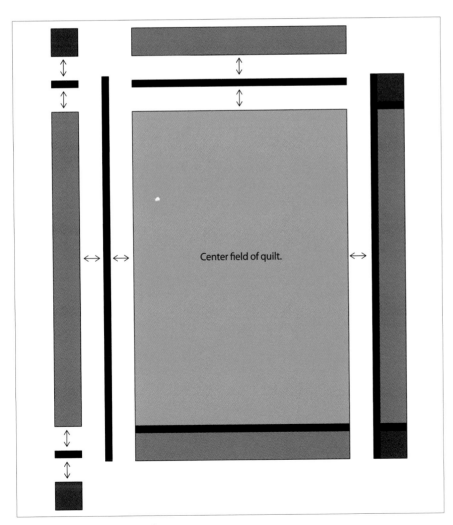

Center field of quilt.

Piecing Sequence for Rebel Borders

GALLERY

Heart of the Arctic *Pieced by the author, machine quilted by Wanda Rains (69" × 69").*

Like Zigzag Zinnias (page 111), what began as a project quilt rapidly became too complicated, with nine different block types and a total of 64 blocks. I could not have designed this without the aid of Electric Quilt® software. My start fabric was the floral print, from which I pulled the other colors, then added the pink as an extra to inject more life and variety.

Antigua *Pieced by Maggie Magee, machine quilted by Wanda Rains (69" × 69").*

In this 64-block quilt, the 36 central blocks are in the Quadrangle setting and appear to come forward against a background of the outer blocks. The yellow shallow triangles in the border provide a wonderful frame for the piece. The warm colors and batik fabric reminded quilter Maggie Magee of her trip to the town of Antigua in Guatemala.

Growing Sunshine *Pieced by Keitha Unger,*
machine quilted by Wanda Rains (68" × 68").

Here is the same Quadrangle setting
found in the center of Antigua (facing
page), but how different it looks on-
point. The brown really pops and creates
a striking pattern where all the small
squares come together. It provides a
lively contrast to the yellow and the
sunflowers. The two elements balance,
giving a pleasing overall pattern that
is further enhanced by the beautiful
curly quilting pattern.

Primrose *Pieced by Andrea Rudman,
machine quilted by Julie Goodwin (66" × 66").*

*This colorful 64-block quilt is presented in the Card Trick setting. Andrea Rudman used fat quarters to make six each of ten block types and four of one type for the corners. Each primrose grouping of three appears twice. The **A1** squares have been subdivided into a small yellow square for the flower center, and a darker rectangle and square. The checkerboard and dark fabrics in the corners of the blocks define the boundaries between the primroses; and the small yellow **D4** square joins with the yellow square in the subdivided **A1**, making the shape of the centers more realistic and less angular.*

126

Bargello Hearts   *Pieced by Linda Gentry, machine quilted by Cindy Paulsgrove (68" × 53").*

*In this 54-block quilt, presented in a staggered (or offset) setting, alternate rows are offset by ¾", the width of the **D** segment. Leftovers from the **A** and **D** strip sets are used to fill in spaces at the ends of the rows. This dynamic arrangement makes entirely new secondary patterns and gives the quilt a unique twist. The border of spaced squares makes an attractive edging for the center field of blocks.*

chapter 7

ENLARGE THE BLOCK

When the block is enlarged from 7" to 9½", the quilt grows quickly. The two project bed quilts each contain less than 40 Bargello blocks, so they are relatively fast to piece.

In Edwardian Garden (photo opposite and page 130), the blocks are set squarely with sashing. Fussy-cutting of the **A1** floral squares adds to the visual impact of the quilt.

In Mississippi Sunflowers (page 136), the blocks are on-point, with plain setting squares added. The beautiful quilting pattern visible in the setting squares and triangles greatly enhances the quilt.

The Bargello block technique remains the same for the larger block, but the strip sizes and counter-cuts are wider. See the 9½" block diagram in Appendix 2 (page 145); and the metric measurements chart in Appendix 4 (page 147).

All strips are cut as follows:

A1, B1, C1, D1 – 4½"
A2, B2, C2, D2 – 3¼"
A3, B3, C3, D3 – 2¼"
A4, B4, C4, D4 – 1½"

Counter-cuts for the segments are: **A** set 4½", **B** set 3¼", **C** set 2¼" and **D** set 1½".

The yield of segments from cutting one full-width strip set (40") is eight for the **A** set, 12 for the **B** set, 16 for the **C** set and 26 for the **D** set.

Edwardian Garden Pieced by the author, machine quilted by Wanda Rains (88" x 88").

Edwardian Garden: 36 Enlarged Blocks

FUSSY-CUTS AND SASHING • QUILT SIZE: 88" × 88" • BLOCK SIZE: 9½"

MATERIALS LIST

- 3 yards beige large floral for blocks, sashing and borders
- 2½ yards blue leaves for sashing, cornerstones, borders and binding
- ¾ yard blue bird floral for blocks
- 1 yard burgundy for blocks and sashing
- 1⅓ yards brown for blocks, cornerstones and borders
- ½ yard gold leaves for blocks
- ¾ yard dark green for blocks

- 1 yard light green leaves for blocks, sashing and cornerstones
- ¾ yard cream for blocks and cornerstones
- ⅔ yard bright blue for blocks and cornerstones
- 1 yard black for blocks and cornerstones
- ⅔ yard orange for blocks
- ¼ yard sand leaves for blocks
- 92" × 92" batting
- 92" × 92" backing fabric

Add elegance and color to a bedroom with this luscious Edwardian-style floral bed quilt. It will look beautiful with antique furnishings and wood floors, adding grace and charm to the room.

Find a large floral theme print that you would love to highlight and draw all the colors from it to complete your fabric palette. The rewards of the finer patterns created by careful fussy-cutting are worth the additional time and attention to detail.

The 36 large blocks are easy to piece, but the quilt is complex, with five block types, sashing strips and fussy-cut **A1** squares. The center sashing strips are also fussy-cut to link the floral **A1** squares. You can simplify the pattern by choosing not to fussy-cut these parts. The sashing strip and cornerstone fabrics are care-fully selected to form an integral part of the overall design.

Read all the directions carefully and make sure you understand them before starting. This project is not recommended for beginners.

Bargello Block Diagram

A1	B1	C1	D1
A2	B2	C2	D2
A3	B3	C3	D3
A4	B4	C4	D4

Constructing Edwardian Garden
(See the cutting charts on pages 132-135.)

1. Cut strips and piece the 36 blocks in the order listed in the cutting instructions: 12 outer corner blocks, 4 inner corner blocks, 4 center floral blocks, 8 outer side blocks and 8 inner side blocks, as instructed in Chapter Two. For block types with only 4 blocks, you can economize on fabric for the **C** and **D** sets by using partial strips.

2. For the 12 outer corner blocks, you should have 2 **A** strip sets, and 1 each of sets **B**, **C** and **D**. For all the other block types, there will be 1 of each strip set, with two exceptions: 1) The **A** segments for the inner corner floral blocks may be cut from the outer corner floral blocks' leftover **A** set. 2) The **D** segments for outer side blocks may be cut from the outer corner floral blocks' leftover **D** set.

3. Counter-cut the **A** sets 4½", the **B** sets 3¼", the **C** sets 2¼" and the **D** set 1½"—the appropriate number for each block type. If you opt to fussy-cut the **A1** squares separately for the inner and outer floral corner blocks and center floral blocks, complete sections of the blocks as instructed on page 39. Your **A** segments will consist of **A2**, **A3** and **A4**, with separate **A1** squares; and the completed **B**, **C** and **D** segments should be joined into one piece.

Four Center Floral Blocks
*With fussy-cut **A1** squares and sashing strips.*

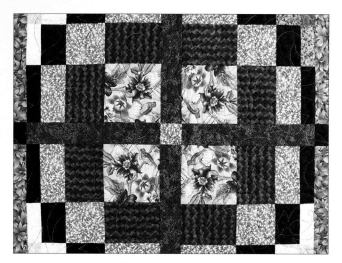

Corner Grouping of Four Blocks

4. First cut the 4 outer border strips (86" × 2½") lengthwise from the blue leaves fabric. Next cut the sashing strips and cornerstones as shown in the table at right. Lay out the blocks (and partial blocks if **A1** squares were fussy-cut), sashing strips and cornerstones in the desired configuration; use the photograph as a guide or make your own pattern. Assemble the center field of the quilt, joining the components in rows (see page 46).

CUTTING FOR SASHING STRIPS AND CORNERSTONES

Fabric	No. of Sashing Strips 10" × 2"	No. of Corner-stones 2" × 2"
Blue Leaves	48	1
Burgundy	24	4
Pale Green Leaves	8	4
Beige Large Floral (option: fussy-cut)	4	0
Black	0	20
Bright Blue	0	12
Brown	0	4
Cream	0	4
Totals	84	49

CUTTING FOR BORDERS

Fabric	Border Part	Quantity	Size	Notes
Beige Large Floral	Side Panels	4	65" × 6½"	See option in Step 5
	Corner Squares	4	6½" × 6½"	Option: fussy-cut
Brown	Edgings for Side Panels	8	65" × 1½"	
	Frames for Corner Squares	8	6½" × 1½"	
		8	8½" × 1½"	
Blue Leaves	Sashing Strips	8	8½" × 2"	
	Outer Borders	4	84" × 2½"	Trim strips already cut
Bright Blue	Outer Border Cornerstones	4	2½" × 2½"	

5. The quilt top should measure 68" × 68" across the center. If the measurement is different, adjust the length of the border strips accordingly (see page 48). Cut the border pieces as shown in the table on the facing page. **Option:** Cut the beige large floral panels longer than necessary initially. This enables you to manipulate the positioning of the print in the panel and to trim to the correct length.

Detail of Border

6. Piece the borders to complete the quilt top. Cut 16 full-width strips from the brown fabric and piece them to make the eight 65" side panel edgings. Sandwich each side panel between 2 brown edgings. Add the blue leaves sashing strips to the ends of the panels. Frame the corner squares with brown, first attaching the 6½" strips to the sides, then the 8½" strips to the tops and bottoms.

Stitch 2 of the side panel sections onto opposite sides of the quilt top. To the other 2, join the framed corner squares onto each end, then sew them onto the top and bottom of the quilt top. Finish the quilt top with the outer border, first joining the sides, then the top and bottom strips with cornerstones. Use the detailed photograph of the quilt border and corner above as an additional guide.

7. Baste, quilt and bind as directed in Chapter One. Edwardian Garden has a soft allover quilting pattern of flowers and leaves that complements the antique floral theme.

Outer Corner Floral Block
Required: 12 blocks.

CUTTING FOR 12 OUTER CORNER FLORAL BLOCKS

Note: Cut strips across the full width of the fabric, selvage to selvage (40").

Option: Fussy-cut 4 sets of 4 **A1** squares exactly the same from the beige large floral print (4½" × 4½"). One of each of these 4 sets of **A1** squares will be used for the 4 inner corner floral blocks (page 134).

Fabric	Block Part	No. of Strips	Size
Beige Large Floral*	**A1**	1	4½" × 40"
Dark Green	**A2**	1	3¼" × 40"
	B1	1	4½" × 40"
Light Green Leaves	**A3**	1	2¼" × 40"
	B2	1	3¼" × 40"
	C1	1	4½" × 40"
Black	**A4**	1	1½" × 40"
	B3	1	2¼" × 40"
	C2	1	3¼" × 40"
	D1	1	4½" × 40"
Cream	**B4**	1	1½" × 40"
	C3	1	2¼" × 40"
	D2	1	3¼" × 40"
Sand Leaves	**C4**	1	1½" × 40"
	D3	1	2¼" × 40"
Gold Leaves	**D4**	1	1½" × 40"

Inner Corner Floral Block
Required: 4 blocks.

Center Floral Block
Required: 4 blocks.

CUTTING FOR 4 INNER CORNER FLORAL BLOCKS

Note: Cut strips across the full width of the fabric, selvage to selvage (40").

For the **A** segments, use the leftover **A** set from the 12 outer corner floral blocks.

*Option: Use the **A1** squares already fussy-cut; see 12 outer corner floral blocks on page 133.

Fabric	Block Part	No. of Strips	Size
Dark Green	**B1**	1	4½" × 40"
Light Green Leaves	**B2**	1	3¼" × 40"
	C1	1	4½" × 40"
Black	**B3**	1	2¼" × 40"
	C2	1	3¼" × 40"
	D1	1	4½" × 40"
Orange	**B4**	1	1½" × 40"
	C3	1	2¼" × 40"
	D2	1	3¼" × 40"
Bright Blue	**C4**	1	1½" × 40"
	D3	1	2¼" × 40"
Cream	**D4**	1	1½" × 40"

CUTTING FOR 4 CENTER FLORAL BLOCKS

Note: Cut strips across the full width of the fabric, selvage to selvage (40").

*Option: Fussy-cut the 4 **A1** squares exactly the same from the beige large floral 4½" × 4½".

Fabric	Block Part	No. of Strips	Size
Beige Large Floral*	**A1**	1	4½" × 40"
Burgundy	**A2**	1	3¼" × 40"
	B1	1	4½" × 40"
Blue Bird Floral	**A3**	1	2¼" × 40"
	B2	1	3¼" × 40"
	C1	1	4½" × 40"
Brown	**A4**	1	1½" × 40"
	B3	1	2¼" × 40"
	C2	1	3¼" × 40"
	D1	1	4½" × 40"
Gold Leaves	**B4**	1	1½" × 40"
	C3	1	2¼" × 40"
	D2	1	3¼" × 40"
Dark Green	**C4**	1	1½" × 40"
	D3	1	2¼" × 40"
Light Green Leaves	**D4**	1	1½" × 40"

Outer Side Block
Required: 8 blocks.

Inner Side Block
Required: 8 blocks.

CUTTING FOR 8 OUTER SIDE BLOCKS

Note: Cut strips across the full width of the fabric, selvage to selvage (40").

For the **D** segments, use the leftover **D** set from the 12 outer corner floral blocks.

Fabric	Block Part	No. of Strips	Size
Bright Blue	A1	1	4½" × 40"
Blue Bird Floral	A2	1	3¼" × 40"
	B1	1	4½" × 40"
Orange	A3	1	2¼" × 40"
	B2	1	3¼" × 40"
	C1	1	4½" × 40"
Black	A4	1	1½" × 40"
	B3	1	2¼" × 40"
	C2	1	3¼" × 40"
Cream	B4	1	1½" × 40"
	C3	1	2¼" × 40"
Sand Leaves	C4	1	1½" × 40"

CUTTING FOR 8 INNER SIDE BLOCKS

Note: Cut strips across the full width of the fabric, selvage to selvage (40").

Fabric	Block Part	No. of Strips	Size
Blue Bird Floral	A1	1	4½" × 40"
Bright Blue	A2	1	3¼" × 40"
	B1	1	4½" × 40"
Cream	A3	1	2¼" × 40"
	B2	1	3¼" × 40"
	C1	1	4½" × 40"
Burgundy	A4	1	1½" × 40"
	B3	1	2¼" × 40"
	C2	1	3¼" × 40"
	D1	1	4½" × 40"
Gold Leaves	B4	1	1½" × 40"
	C3	1	2¼" × 40"
	D2	1	3¼" × 40"
Dark Green	C4	1	1½" × 40"
	D3	1	2¼" × 40"
Light Green Leaves	D4	1	1½" × 40"

Mississippi Sunflowers. Pieced by the author, machine quilted by Wanda Rains (96¼" × 83").
Photo by Mark Frey.

Mississippi Sunflowers: 38 Enlarged Blocks

QUILT SIZE: 96¼" × 83" • BLOCK SIZE: 9½"

MATERIALS LIST

- 1½ yards orange batik for blocks, setting squares and borders
- 3 yards sunflowers batik for blocks, borders and binding
- ½ yard purple batik for blocks
- 1¼ yards blue cloud batik for blocks
- ¾ yard rust flower batik for blocks
- ½ yard rust feather batik for blocks
- 1¼ yards cream I batik for blocks

- ½ yard cream II batik for setting squares
- 2¼ yards black swirl batik for blocks, setting and corner triangles
- ⅓ yard blue mono batik for blocks
- 102" × 88" batting
- 102" × 88" backing fabric

This bold, vibrant bed quilt is a lively focal point that brings the sunshine indoors. The striking pattern is beautifully enhanced and balanced by intricate quilting patterns in the plain setting squares and triangles. Additional texture and richness abound in the natural variations within the batik fabrics.

This large quilt is quick to piece with only 38 Bargello blocks—22 of one block type and 16 of another. The two block types are almost identical, the only differences being in the **A3-B2-C1** rust arc and **A1** squares. The two rust fabrics are similar in color but differ in texture, adding more depth and interest to the pattern.

The quilt was a wedding gift to a special young couple living in Mississippi; hence the name, Mississippi Sunflowers.

A1	B1	C1	D1
A2	B2	C2	D2
A3	B3	C3	D3
A4	B4	C4	D4

Bargello Block Diagram

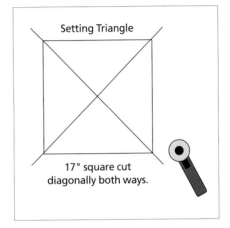

Setting Triangle

17" square cut diagonally both ways.

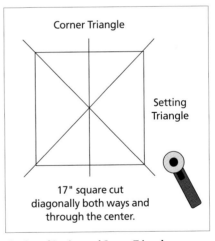

Corner Triangle

Setting Triangle

17" square cut diagonally both ways and through the center.

Cutting of Setting and Corner Triangles

Constructing Mississippi Sunflowers
(See the cutting charts on pages 138-139.)

1. Piece the 38 blocks: 22 rust flower blocks and 16 rust feather blocks, as directed in Chapter Two. For the rust flower block type, you should have 3 **A** strip sets, 2 **B** and **C** sets and 1 **D** set. For the rust feather block type, there are 2 strip sets for **A** and **B**, and 1 each for **C** and **D**. Counter-cut the **A** sets 4½", the **B** sets 3¼", the **C** sets 2¼" and the **D** set 1½": 22 segments of each for the rust flower blocks and 16 of each for the rust feather blocks. Cut the **A1** squares separately as directed in the cutting table, and complete sections of the blocks as instructed on page 39. Your **A** segments will consist of **A2**, **A3** and **A4**, with separate **A1** squares. The completed **B**, **C** and **D** segments should be joined into 1 piece.

2. Cut the 8 orange and 4 cream II setting squares (10" × 10"). For the black swirl setting and corner triangles, cut five 17" squares. Divide 4 of them into quarters by cutting diagonally in both directions to yield 16 setting triangles. Cut the fifth in the same way, then cut 2 of the triangles in half, to yield 2 more setting triangles and 4 corner triangles as shown in the illustration above.

3. Lay out the block segments and **A1** squares in the desired configuration with the setting squares, triangles and corners; use the photograph as a guide or make your own pattern. You can experiment by cutting different **A1** squares to create a new look. Join the **A1** squares onto the **A** segments, then complete the blocks.

4. Assemble the center field of the quilt, joining the components in diagonal rows (see page 46). Trim away the excess from the sides, leaving ¼" seam allowances all the way around (see page 47). The center field should measure approximately 80¼" × 67".

5. Cut 9 full-width 2" orange border strips and join them to make 88" strips for the sides and 74" strips for the top and bottom. Cut the 7" sunflower outer borders down the length of the fabric, allowing 102" for the sides and 88" for the top and bottom. Center the orange strips on the sunflower strips and sew them together, then join them to the quilt top, mitering the corners (see page 48).

6. Baste, quilt and bind as directed in Chapter One. Mississippi Sunflowers has a wealth of beautiful quilting patterns over the surface. The complex curly suns complement the sunflower fabric perfectly and look spectacular, especially on the dark setting triangles and corners.

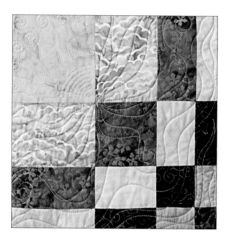

Rust Flower/Orange Block
Required: 12 blocks.

Rust Flower/Purple Block
Required: 10 blocks.

CUTTING FOR 22 RUST FLOWER BLOCKS

Note: Cut strips across the full width of the fabric, selvage to selvage (40").

Cut the **A1** squares separately: 10 purple and 12 orange (4½" × 4½").

Fabric	Block Part	No. of Strips	Size
Blue Cloud	A2	3	3¼" × 40"
	B1	2	4½" × 40"
Rust Flower	A3	3	2¼" × 40"
	B2	2	3¼" × 40"
	C1	2	4½" × 40"
Cream 1	A4	3	1½" × 40"
	B3	2	2¼" × 40"
	C2	2	3¼" × 40"
	D1	1	4½" × 40"
Black Swirl	B4	2	1½" × 40"
	C3	2	2¼" × 40"
	D2	1	3¼" × 40"
Blue Mono	C4	2	1½" × 40"
	D3	1	2¼" × 40"
Purple	D4	1	1½" × 40"

Rust Feather/Sunflower Block

Required: 4 blocks.

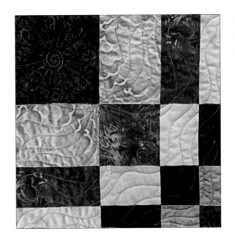

Rust Feather/Purple Block

Required: 4 blocks.

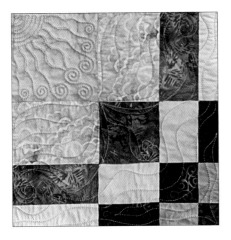

Rust Feather/Orange Block

Required: 8 blocks.

CUTTING FOR 16 RUST FEATHER BLOCKS

Note: Cut strips across the full width of the fabric, selvage to selvage (40").

Cut the **A1** squares separately: 4 sunflower, 4 purple and 8 orange (4½" × 4½").

Fabric	Block Part	No. of Strips	Size
Blue Cloud	A2	2	3¼" × 40"
	B1	2	4½" × 40"
Rust Feather	A3	2	2¼" × 40"
	B2	2	3¼" × 40"
	C1	1	4½" × 40"
Cream 1	A4	2	1½" × 40"
	B3	2	2¼" × 40"
	C2	1	3¼" × 40"
	D1	1	4½" × 40"
Black Swirl	B4	2	1½" × 40"
	C3	1	2¼" × 40"
	D2	1	3¼" × 40"
Blue Mono	C4	1	1½" × 40"
	D3	1	2¼" × 40"
Purple	D4	1	1½" × 40"

Quilting Detail on Mississippi Sunflowers (left and right) *Photos by Mark Frey.*

GALLERY

Citrus Delight   *Pieced by Kelma Jo Burns, machine quilted by Wanda Rains (74" × 58").*

This bright and cheerful quilt has 48 blocks in the Quadrangle setting. The green and yellow strips almost look like a triple sashing, but they are, of course, parts of the blocks. This is a simple squarely set quilt with no sashing strips.

Bargello with a Twist of Orange *Made by Gladys Schulz (98" × 85").*

*In this stunning bed quilt, the on-point blocks are grouped in fours with orange sashing strips. These groupings are then set together with black sashing strips and yellow cornerstones. All 50 blocks are the same, but the large print in the **A1** squares provides variations between the blocks.*

Appendix 1

7" Bargello Block Diagram with Cutting Sizes of Strips

A1 – 3½"	B1 – 3½"	C1 – 3½"	D1 – 3½"
A2 – 2½"	B2 – 2½"	C2 – 2½"	D2 – 2½"
A3 – 1¾"	B3 – 1¾"	C3 – 1¾"	D3 – 1¾"
A4 – 1¼"	B4 – 1¼"	C4 – 1¼"	D4 – 1¼"

Enlarge by 164%

Appendix 2

9½" Bargello Block Diagram with Cutting Sizes of Strips

A1 – 4½"	B1 – 4½"	C1 – 4½"	D1 – 4½"
A2 – 3¼"	B2 – 3¼"	C2 – 3¼"	D2 – 3¼"
A3 – 2¼"	B3 – 2¼"	C3 – 2¼"	D3 – 2¼"
A4 – 1½"	B4 – 1½"	C4 – 1½"	D4 – 1½"

Enlarge by 164%

Appendix 3

Fabric Cutting Plan

Fabric (describe)_____

Set A   Set C

Set B   Set D

Fabric_____

Set A   Set C

Set B   Set D

Fabric_____

Set A   Set C

Set B   Set D

Fabric_____

Set A   Set C

Set B   Set D

Fabric_____

Set A   Set C

Set B   Set D

Fabric_____

Set A   Set C

Set B   Set D

Fabric_____

Set A   Set C

Set B   Set D

Appendix 4

Metric Measurements for Bargello Blocks

Use a consistent seam allowance of 0.75cm. The 7" Bargello block converts to 17.5cm and the enlarged 9½" block to 24cm.

CUTTING SIZES FOR 17.5CM AND 24CM BLOCKS		
Strips	**17.5cm Block**	**24cm Block**
A1, B1, C1, D1	9.0cm	11.5cm
A2, B2, C2, D2	6.5cm	8.5cm
A3, B3, C3, D3	4.5cm	6.0cm
A4, B4, C4, D4	3.0cm	4.0cm
Counter-cuts for segments	**17.5cm Block**	**24cm Block**
Set **A**	9.0cm	11.5cm
Set **B**	6.5cm	8.5cm
Set **C**	4.5cm	6.0cm
Set **D**	3.0cm	4.0cm

Appendix 5

Annotated 7" Bargello Block Diagram

**Bargello Block
Diagram**

A1	B1	C1	D1
A2	B2	C2	D2
A3	B3	C3	D3
A4	B4	C4	D4

Appendix 6

Example of Completed Fabric Cutting Plan for Bargello Block Diagram in Appendix 5

Fabric (describe) Feathers   (16 blocks)

Set A A1 – 3½" x 2   Set C C3 – 1¾"

Set B B2 – 2½"   Set D D4 – 1¼"

Fabric Gold Wings

Set A A2 – 2½" x 2   Set C

Set B B1 – 3½"   Set D

Fabric Dark Brown

Set A A3 – 1¾" x 2   Set C C1 – 3½"

Set B   Set D

Fabric Lime Green

Set A A4 – 1¼" x 2   Set C C2 – 2½"

Set B B3 – 1¾"   Set D D1 – 3½"

Fabric Rust

Set A   Set C

Set B B4 – 1¼"   Set D D2 – 2½"

Fabric Light Beige

Set A   Set C C4 – 1¼"

Set B   Set D D3 – 1¾"

Fabric

Set A   Set C

Set B   Set D

Appendix 7

Line Diagram of Deck of Pansies (36 Blocks; page 74)

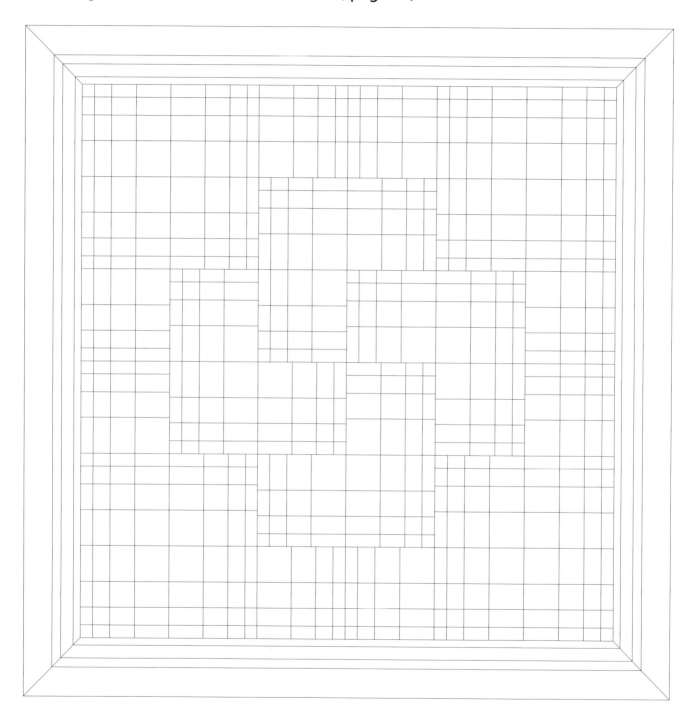

Appendix 8

Line Diagram of Bainbridge Delft (24 Blocks On-Point; page 92)

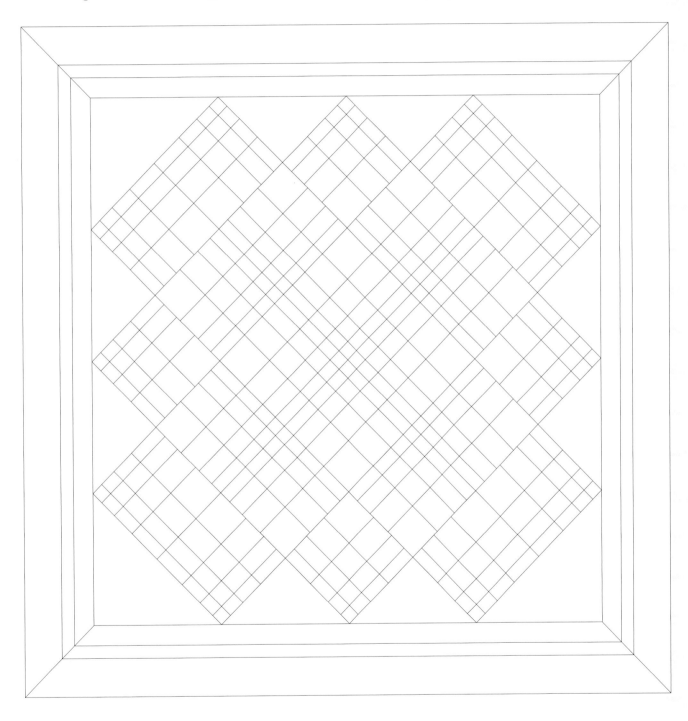

Bargello Circles Pieced by Linda Johnston.

Quilt Contributors

Many thanks to my students and quilting friends for sharing their beautiful quilts in this book. A special thank-you goes to Wanda Rains, who machine quilted eight of the following quilts and 20 of my 22 quilts.

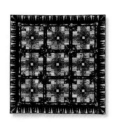

Marilyn Ahnemiller
Safari Quilt
page 88

Klina Dupuy
A Few Flowers for the Garden
page 67

Linda Gentry
Bargello Hearts
page 127

Joanne Bennett
Swimming in Circles
page 108

Klina Dupuy
Twist of Glitz
page 110

Carol Graves
Bubble Gum Confection
page 64

Kelma Jo Burns
Citrus Delight
page 142

Penny Evers
Summer Lime
page 109

Michelle Hoel
Forest Flowers
page 87

Lisa Jenni
Floral Tropicana
page 87

Carol McKim
Purple Passion
pages 4-5, 111

Gladys Schulz
Bargello with a Twist of Orange
pages 11, 143

Christine Johnson
Destination
page 66

Barbara Micheal
Buon Natale
page 62

Pam Syracuse
Field of Flowers
page 114

Christine Johnson
Reflections
page 82

Jacque Noard
Garden Picnic
page 84

Keitha Unger
Growing Sunshine
page 125

Linda Johnston
Bargello Circles
pages 62, 152

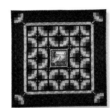

Wanda Rains
Wolf Reflections
page 89

Anita Webb
Gecko Madness
page 108

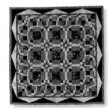

Maggie Magee
Antigua
page 124

Andrea Rudman
Primroses
page 126

Carol Wood
Fishgello
pages 6, 84

Valerie Martinson
Mom's Heavenly Garden
page 66

Gladys Schulz
American Hero's Bargello
page 100

Supply Sources

Batting

Fairfield Processing
P.O. Box 1157
Danbury, CT 06813-1157
(800) 980-8000
www.poly-fil.com

Commercial Machine Quilting

Wanda Rains
Rainy Day Quilts
22448 NE Jefferson Point Road
Kingston, WA 98346
(360) 297-5115
www.rainydayquilts.com

Computer Software for Quilters

The Electric Quilt Company®
419 Gould Street, Suite 2
Bowling Green, OH 43402-3047
(800) 356-4219
www.electricquilt.com

Decorative Threads

Sulky of America
980 Cobb Place Blvd., Suite 130
Kennesaw, GA 30144
(800) 874-4115
www.sulky.com

Fabric

David Textiles, Inc.
1920 S. Tubeway Avenue
City of Commerce, CA 90040
(800) 548-1818

Mats, Rotary Cutters and Rulers

Prym-Dritz Corporation
P.O. Box 5028
Spartanburg, SC 29304
(800) 845-4948
www.dritz.com

Mitering Ruler

From Marti Michell
P.O. Box 80218
Atlanta, GA 30366
(800) 558-3568
www.frommarti.com

Quilt Photography

Mark Frey
P.O. Box 1596
Yelm, WA 98597
(360) 894-3591

Sewing Machines

VSM Sewing, Inc.
31000 Viking Parkway
Westlake, OH 44145
(800) 358-0001
www.husqvarnaviking.com

Threads

Coats & Clark
Consumer Services
P.O. Box 12229
Greenville, SC 29612-0229
(800) 648-1479
www.coatsandclark.com

About the Author

Maggie Ball has over 20 years of experience quilting. Her award-winning quilts have been exhibited both nationally and internationally. She teaches quilting to all ages and has traveled twice to Mongolia as a volunteer to teach unemployed and low-income women.

Maggie, a native of England, lives with her family on Bainbridge Island in the Pacific Northwest. *Bargello Quilts with a Twist* is Maggie's fourth book. Her previous three, *Creative Quilting with Kids*, *Patchwork and Quilting with Kids* and *Traditional Quilts with a Twist* were published by Krause Publications in 2001, 2003 and 2006 respectively.

For further information and to request Maggie to teach at quilt guilds, retreats and conferences, visit her website at www.dragonflyquilts.com.

Heart of the Arctic   Pieced by the author, machine quilted by Wanda Rains.

Index

More Great Ideas for Twisting Tradition

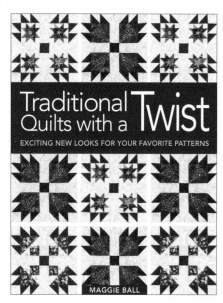

Use traditional quilt blocks to create unique variations through more than 20 projects demonstrated in 200+ color photos. Paperback, 128 pages, #TRQV.
ISBN-10: 0-89689-273-5
ISBN-13: 978-0-89689-273-6

Using the fun, pinless and foolproof 3-6-9 System you'll discover endless quilt design possibilities within your reach. Includes bonus CD featuring appliqué templates and embroidery designs. Paperback, 128 pages, #Z0996.
ISBN-10: 0-89689-559-9
ISBN-13: 978-0-89689-559-1

Discover a new twist on traditional quilting, and showcase individuality with the clever "freedom block" approach demonstrated in 15 step-by-step projects, 300 color photos and appliqué patterns. Paperback, 128 pages, #LCQA.
ISBN-10: 0-89689-308-1
ISBN-13: 978-0-89689-308-5

Discover the rewards of learning to translate an ancient pattern into beautiful pieced patchwork designs in this exciting book, which turns an interesting mathematical phenomenon into a beautiful quilt design. Paperback, 128 pages, #41865. **ISBN-10: 0-7153-1941-8**
ISBN-13: 978-0-7153-1941-3

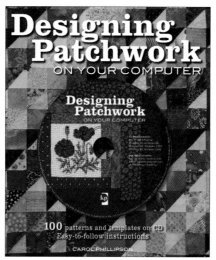

This book/CD combo provides you with step-by-step instructions for designing a wide range of patchwork blocks, using just a few keystrokes. Hardcover, 128 pages, #Z0755.
ISBN-10: 0-89689-400-2
ISBN-13: 978-0-89689-400-6